CENTRAL COLORADO SKI TOURS

Colorado Springs
Denver
Fairplay
Leadville
Salida
Gunnison
Crested Butte
Aspen
Glenwood Springs
Grand Junction

D0034137

By Tom and Sanse Sudduth

PRUETT **P** PUBLISHING COMPANY
Boulder, Colorado

Library of Congress Catalog Card No. 77-91914

First Edition
 2 3 4 5 6 7 8 9

ISBN: 0-87108-518-6

Winter Backcountry Ethics and *Glossary* courtesy
The Touchstone Press, Beaverton, Oregon.

PREFACE

I climbed slowly and steadily up the snowy-white basin, making long switchbacks to gain the 11,700-foot top of Taylor Hill northeast of Tennessee Pass. Ahead Jim Gregg and Bryan DeBenedetti of the Holy Cross Ranger District broke trail — plotting a course for the new Trail of the Tenth (No. 12) — behind, Sanse and then Bob Newman of the Leadville District followed the tracks, and I was glad both for the trail-breaking and the company. As we neared the first high ridge, rugged, pristine-white Sawatch Peaks rose on the skyline behind, a contrast to the smooth banks of Chicago Ridge right. In several more hundred yards a dazzling vista of Holy Cross Peaks, distant Flattops, jagged spires in the Gore Range, and finally, white summits of the Tenmile Range, all spread out along the skyline, forming one of the most incredible wintertime vistas I had seen in Colorado. From the summit of Taylor Pass, we descended northwest beneath a thick canopy of evergreens, the view suddenly cut off, and the mood quiet and intimate. We followed a compass bearing to stay on course, exploded small patches of powder snow on the steep drops, and contorted into strange positions to escape the tree branches. And at the trail's end, I had this exhilarating feeling: "Here is the best ski tour in central Colorado!"

It was a feeling that I would have again and again as Sanse and I researched the tour routes for this book. Again upon seeing the towering Collegiate Peaks across the flat bed of Taylor Park Reservoir (No. 23) and again after climbing the Express Creek Road (No. 36) to a top-of-the-world vista of the striated summits in the Elk Mountains. Each tour, in fact, produced its own special demands and gave its unique rewards: awesomeness of the wind-blown Fourteeners in the Mosquito Range and beauty of the ancient, battle-worn bristlecone pine on the Bristlecone Pine Scenic Area tour (No. 8), grandeur of snow-capped Mount Sopris on the Dinkle and Thomas Lakes tour (No. 44), loneliness and apprehension on the tour into the Dark Canyon (No. 47), and sheer delight in skiing on all the Grand Mesa tours (No's. 53-58).

This book is an invitation to ski the trails of central Colorado, and to experience the grandeur, the exhilaration, and the loneliness of the backcountry in winter.

SKI TOURING IN CENTRAL COLORADO

The general techniques of ski touring and winter camping are not within the scope of this book. Other books cover these subjects well and are highly recommended: *The Regnery Guide To Ski Touring* by Sven Wiik and David Sumner, *Steve Rieschl's Ski-Touring For The Fun Of It* by Cortlandt L. Freeman, and *The Complete Snow Camper's Guide* by Raymond Bridge. In addition, nearly every sizeable town in central Colorado has a number of RMSIA Certified Ski Touring Instructors and Day Tour Leaders. For a list of names and addresses, write the Rocky Mountain Ski Instructors Association, Box 4, Steamboat Springs, CO 80477.

CENTRAL COLORADO RANGES: Each mountain range in central Colorado has its own distinctive features. The massive, rounded Mosquito Range west of South Park, with several summits reaching over 14,000 feet, has the most varied, or undependable, snow conditions. Moderate snow cover drifts into the valleys and banks of trees from December through March but slopes above timberline are often swept bare by the wind. Heavy spring snow adheres to the high tundra and sometimes allows touring in April. The Sawatch Range west of Leadville, Buena Vista and Salida, formed by some of Colorado's highest peaks (for example, Mt. Elbert at 14,433 feet) holds excellent ski touring opportunities throughout the winter and spring, best at Tennessee Pass near the northern end of the range and at Monarch Pass at the southern end. West of Buena Vista, the tour routes follow open roads, are often windy, and have variable snow cover, much like the conditions in the Colorado Front Range. The Elk Mountain Range between Crested Butte and Aspen historically receives the deepest snows in central Colorado. This area offers a range of skiing — commercial with a trail ticket or free on public land, track-skiing or tour-skiing. For strong, intermediate skiers with good downhill technique, steep trails to mountain cabins in the USSA's Alfred E. Braun Hut System provide the ultimate ski touring experience. In this range dry powder fills the valleys and north-facing slopes through March; crusted snow covers the south-facing areas exposed to wind and sun. The Grand Mesa, one of the world's largest flat-topped mountains, rises above dry fields of sage and irrigated farms but has surprisingly one of the longest ski seasons in Colorado, very similar to the Park Range at Rabbit Ears Pass. The terrain rolls gently here and the accent is on skiing rather than on spectacular vistas. Sunrise tours on the hard snow crust are often possible as late as mid-June, with klister wax, glacier goggles, and sun-screen lotion as necessary equipment.

LIFE ZONES: On any particular ski route the most useful indicator for weather and snow conditions, and for the type of wildlife, is the life zone or elevation range through which the route travels. In the lower reaches of the Canadian Life Zone (8,000-10,000 feet elevation) mild weather prevails and snow cover melts more rapidly, staying longest along shaded, north-facing slopes. This area offers the best chance of seeing large game such as deer, elk, and even Rocky Mountain Bighorn sheep and Rocky Mountain goats in the Front Range. (Please do not startle big game; observe from a distance. See Winter Backcountry Ethics.) In the Hudsonian Life Zone (10,000 feet elevation to timberline) snow cover is generally dependable from December through April on all hillsides. Although wary and difficult to spot, many small mammals such as coyotes, foxes, cottontail rabbits, and snowshoe hares inhabit this area. In spring especially, the warm, windless days and crusted snowpack create ideal touring and camping conditions in this zone. The Arctic-Alpine Life Zone, from timberline to the tops of the high mountain peaks, holds winter's spell longest, often receiving snow when spring rain falls in the lower regions. Here, white-tailed ptarmigan hide in the wind-stunted brush, while mountain chickadees can be seen in the spruce trees near timberline. Large snowbanks remain through May and early June in this area.

SNOWMOBILE AREAS: In an effort to prevent conflict with snowmobilers, all major snowmobiling areas have been left out of this book, even though the terrain might also be suitable for touring. These areas include the Rampart Range between Denver and Colorado Springs, the Sawatch Range west of Buena Vista, the Black Mesa east of Montrose, and the Lands End section of the Grand Mesa. Tours entitled ''Ski Trails'' are designated by the Forest Service for ski touring and snowshoeing use only and often have an excellent ski track.

THE COLORADO TRAIL: This major trail corridor for summer backpackers and winter ski tourers, closed to motorized vehicles, connects Denver with Durango. Many segments of The Colorado Trail, when completed, will serve as ski tour routes: possibly from Kenosha Pass to the Michigan Creek area (No. 6), and from Tennessee Pass (No. 14) along the east side of the Sawatch Range via the Main Range and other trails to U.S. 50. For more information, contact the Colorado Mountain Trails Foundation, P.O. Box 2238, Littleton, Colorado 80161.

HOW TO USE THIS BOOK

The information capsule which precedes each text lists ten important facts about the tour and provides a means for quick comparison with other tours.

First, tours are divided into half-day trips, one-day trips, and overnights according to the type of terrain, distance, skiing time, etc. from the starting point to the recommended destination. A **half-day trip** allows a morning or afternoon of exercise and fresh air and measures about 2.5 miles or less one way, sometimes more when the tour follows a downhill, and hence faster, course. A **one-day trip** usually reaches the destination for a lunch stop, and then returns over the ski tracks or makes a loop return, a trip taking the greater part of a day. An **overnight** proceeds to a suggested point too far into the backcountry to allow a safe return in the same day and thus requires sleeping bag, tent or snowcave shovel, other winter camping equipment, and food.

Next, the **terrain** is rated, following the criteria now used for ski touring trails in National Forests throughout the United States. In general, **Easiest** tour routes (coded on signs with a green circle) have no downhill or uphill runs over a 10 percent slope. Downhill sections have smooth surfaces and gentle, sweeping turns and outruns have ample space to slow down before turning again. **More difficult** tour routes (blue square) have downhill and uphill sections over 10 percent and under 50 percent slope but the steeper sections are very short. Tour routes rated **Most difficult** (black diamond) indicate downhill and uphill sections over 30 percent slope with some very steep, 60 to 70 percent sections. ("Intermediate" or "more difficult" **alpine** ski runs average about 40 percent slope.) Rougher terrain, shorter, tighter turns, and shorter run-outs distinguish these routes from Easiest and More difficult routes. The newly-standardized Forest Service trail blazer for designated ski touring trails is a 4"x5" elongated diamond of pale blue (or sometimes international orange) color.

Tour **distance,** listed in both miles and kilometers, is measured very carefully one-way only for tours that return over the same track and total round trip distance for tours that follow a loop return. Steep switchback areas on cross-country trips, both uphill and downhill, are figured as twice their linear distance.

Skiing time, given as a guide only for skiers who are not sure of their pace, corresponds to the one-way or round trip distance. For tours over Easiest terrain, it is calculated at 1-1½ miles per hour, a comfortable rate which allows time for rest stops, rewaxing, picture-taking, etc. For More and Most difficult tours, skiing time is determined from a rate of 2 miles per hour and adjusted according to specific differences in terrain. Lunch breaks and driving time are not included.

Elevation gain or **loss,** listed in both feet and meters, measures the difference between the highest and lowest points on the tour. It is usually the single most important factor in determining tour difficulty. If the route contains significant drops and climbs within its length, each uphill increment is added together for an **accumulated elevation gain,** each downhill increment added together for an **accumulated elevation loss.**

Each life zone or elevation range holds unique and predictable rewards and hazards for ski touring, a topic reviewed in *Ski Touring in Central Colorado* (see above). The **maximum elevation** or highest point along the tour route is a useful indicator of these conditions.

Except for the Front Range and Mosquito Range areas, the amount of snowfall remains fairly constant from year to year in the central Colorado mountains, although several factors such as wind exposure, side of the hill, elevation range, and even skier-use determine snow conditions on a specific route. The **season** listed for each tour suggests those months where adequate snow covers the trail to insure good skiing conditions. This information represents a consensus of Forest Service personnel and experienced ski tourers.

All appropriate **U.S.G.S. topographic maps** and their publication dates are listed in the order that the tour route crosses them. These maps provide extremely useful information for ski touring, especially for the longer and more difficult tour routes. Based on aerial photographs, they show the shape and elevation of the terrain, plot major trails, roads, creeks, and lakes, and differentiate between woodland, scrub, and open areas. U.S.G.S. topo maps are available for purchase at most mountaineering shops or may be obtained from the U.S. government by sending the map name and $1.25 to the Central Region-Map Distribution, U.S. Geological Survey, Denver Federal Center, Bldg. 41, Denver, Colorado 80225.

And, as final items in the information capsule, the relevant **Ranger District** and **National Forest** are given to help place the tour geographically and to identify a source of further information.

Each ski tour text is organized into a paragraph or two of introduction, a paragraph of driving directions, and several paragraphs of specific trail information. The introduction discusses prominent features of the tour such as interesting history and the origin of place names, spectacular viewpoints, outstanding ski runs, and prevalent hazards. The paragraph of driving directions provides instruction from the nearest town or landmark, suggests a parking area, and notes variable conditions such as likely snowdrifts and unplowed roads. The remaining paragraphs of trail information summarize the tour route and include good vistas, promising alternate routes, unique trail features, and common tree types.

General directions, such as "east-northeast" and "southwest," are based on true north for landmarks as they appear on the topo map rather than on magnetic north as they would read on a compass. Specific directions, such as "152°/SSE," are given when more accurate orientation is needed, listed first with the exact bearing based on magnetic north, then second with the bearing based on true north (magnetic bearing + approx. 14°) and rounded to the sixteen points of the compass. To use the magnetic bearing (with a Silva compass), simply dial the bearing, align the compass needle with the orienting arrow, and look along the direction-of-travel arrowhead.

Specific ski terms such as "glide," "telemark," "double pole," etc. are given in the trail information not to prescribe a certain technique for a certain part of the trail but to provide a better understanding in ski touring language of the terrain.

The map photos in the book, enlarged or reduced sections of U.S.G.S. topo maps used for each tour, correlate closely with the tour description. Symbols that have been drafted onto the map such as "starting point" and "avalanche danger" are listed in the legend. For the best understanding of the tour, read the text and at the same time, follow the trail carefully along the map, noting each prominent feature as described.

WINTER BACKCOUNTRY ETHICS

Although many wilderness areas in central Colorado are never crossed in winter by touring tracks, the more popular trails suffer from crowded parking lots and heavy skier traffic. In these well-used areas the potential for environmental damage is great and each ski tourer must share the responsibility in making the minimum physical and visual impact upon the land. The following list of winter backcountry ethics will help assure that the sport of ski touring will be as enjoyable in the future as it is today.

RESPECT PRIVATE PROPERY. Road closures in winter sometimes create problems of access to public lands and private-but-open lands and problems of sufficient parking area, a situation antagonized by the ever increasing numbers of ski tourers. **Always seek permission before crossing any private land; never assume access; respect "No Trespassing" signs.** Use common-sense consideration in parking at trailheads. Be careful to avoid blocking private driveways and other cars. Also, be self-sufficient in handling car problems and muddy or slick road conditions.

PACK IT OUT. In winter the pristine beauty of the backcountry conveys a particularly refreshing feeling to its viewers, especially when a blanket of new snow covers the ground. Few things mar this natural splendor more than the sight of city-waste, garbage and litter. Make a habit of putting every scrap of trash — bottles, cans, orange peels, tin from wax cans — into a litter bag, then pack it out. **Remember: trash and snow don't mix.**

DO NOT DISTURB WILDLIFE. The influx of ski tourers into elk and deer wintering ranges threatens the survival of these magnificent animals more than do hunters. A startled elk, for example, will often run until exhausted; then wet and overheated, it will die from pneumonia. Or die from starvation and disease, unable to find enough food for its enormous 1000-pound body to replace the precious calories lost while fleeing. Dogs can easily kill elk and deer in winter by simply chasing them. Therefore, observe wildlife from a distance, perhaps with the aid of binoculars. Avoid elk and deer wintering grounds; pass quietly or detour if you should happen to spot some animals. Leave dogs at home.

CAMP WITHOUT A TRACE. Gone are the days of chopping, digging, lashing, splicing woodcraft, of the ingenious backwoods artisan who can fashion three types of firepits and build several assorted tree-bough beds. The goal for nature-sensitive ski tourers today is to camp so simply that later visitors to the site will find no trace of human use. To keep from scarring the environment, use gas stoves and foam pads instead of wood fires and bough beds. Leave the attractive dead branches on the trees.

OBSERVE WILDERNESS SANITATION RULES. Keep in mind that there are no sanitation facilities in the backcountry and make a point of using toilets before beginning the ski tour. If you must relieve yourself, find a screened spot away from travel and water routes, bury all waste, and burn then bury the toilet paper.

KNOW THE HAZARDS. Remember that pain, anguish, frustration, and despair belong to the world of man. **The mountains don't care.** Every ski tourer who enters the backcountry takes with him the individual responsibility for his comfort and safety. Know the symptoms and prevention of hypothermia; learn proper route selection around potential avalanche sites; become skilled with map and compass in case of disorientation or white-out conditions. Rescue parties frequently must endure severe risks — often unnecessary if those needing help had taken the basic precautions. ...Educate others in the winter backcountry ethics; ski softly in the wilderness and...

PLEASE LEAVE NOTHING BUT YOUR SKI TRACKS.

AVALANCHE RECOGNITION AND RULES

Several trails in central Colorado, although toured occasionally by seasoned ski tourers who can judge the risk, have been omitted from this book due to unacceptable avalanche hazard. These include the Independence Pass summit, Conundrum Pass Trail, East Maroon Pass Trail, and West Maroon Pass Trail. Other touring trails such as Gothic (No. 32) have been included with warnings on the avalanche danger and with a conscientious effort to identify on the map photo the most likely slide paths. However, small snowslides vary in specific location, are difficult — if not impossible — to identify on a map, and are generally unpredictable. Each ski tourer must take the individual responsibility of learning basic avalanche recognition and safety rules. For the best source of information, obtain the detailed, illustrated *Avalanche Handbook* by Ronald I. Perla and M. Martinelli, Jr., by requesting Agriculture Handbook 489, from the Superintendent of Documents, U.S. Government Printing Office, Washington, D.C. 20402. Price: $3.95. The following safety procedures and precautions are presented as a guide for touring in areas of potential avalanche.

MAKE OBSERVATIONS BEFORE STARTING. Learn prior weather conditions: cold temperatures mean more unstable snow; warm temperatures (freezing or above) increase snow stability. Snowstorms beginning with cold temperatures and ending with rising temperatures form snowpacks with a poor bond. Sustained winds of 15 m.p.h. or more and snow falling at one inch per hour or more increase greatly the probability of avalanche. Check with the Forest Service Ranger Station or Ski Area ski patrol for avalanche conditions.

SELECT THE SAFEST ROUTE. For generally safe routes, follow the ridgetops on the windward side but away from any cornices or ski the valleys well away from slopes. Never cross beneath a corniced slope and never traverse a dangerous open snowfield. Remember: most avalanche victims trigger the slides in which they are caught.

BE AWARE OF DANGER SIGNALS. Look for and avoid old slide paths where trees have broken off limbs and snow debris has been deposited below. Listen for hollow sounds, particularly on leeward (opposite of windward) slopes, and watch for snow cracks. Beware of conditions when snowballs or "cartwheels" roll down the slope.

OBSERVE AVALANCHE PRECAUTIONS ON POTENTIALLY DANGEROUS CROSSINGS. Position tour group well away from the potential path site. Cross high on the slope; ski quickly and one at a time; trail a brightly-colored avalanche cord or turn on an electronic signaling device. Instruct other members of the group to watch carefully and to physically mark the last seen spot if the slide breaks. The tour group as a search party represents the only real chance for your survival if you are caught. Use natural safety islands such as tree clumps and rock outcroppings for rest stops.

AUTHOR'S NOTE

No guidebook which attempts to identify the best touring trails in central Colorado could hope to succeed without the help of local, veteran ski tourers. To all the exceptional people who traced their favorite trails on the topo maps, described the best approaches, and pointed out the dangers, to our ski touring friends who kept us company along the trails, we give a sincere thanks.

We would like to express our gratitude especially to those who contributed directly to the tour selection and we refer the reader to them for further information. **In Colorado Springs:** Bob Peto of Holubar Mountaineering Ltd. and Bob Willmot of the Pikes Peak Ranger District. **In Denver:** Bob Miller and Chuck McConnell of the Rocky Mountain Regional Office and Mike Spencer of the South Platte Ranger District. **In Fairplay:** Jerry Davis of the South Park Ranger District. **In Minturn:** Jim Gregg of the Holy Cross Ranger District. **In the Arkansas Valley area:** Dan Heinz and Cindy Rivera of the Leadville Ranger District, Warren Hartman of the Salida Ranger District, Al McClelland of Rocky Mountain Expeditions Inc., and Ned Stock of the Monarch Ski Area. **In the Gunnison and Crested Butte areas:** Bernie Weingardt of the Cebolla Ranger District, Bill Kerr, Jim and "Shammy" Somrak of the Taylor River District, Dr. Hugo Ferchau of Western State College, Bill Frame and Ron Hudelson of The Alpineer, and Don West of Freedom of the Hills Ski School. **In Aspen:** Dick Cerise of the Aspen Ranger District, Fred Braun, Chairman of USSA Hut Committee, Jim Ward of Fothergill's Outdoor Sportsman, Lars Larson of Lars Guide Service, Greg Mace of Ashcroft Ski Touring Unlimited and Amund Ekroll of Snowmass Ski Touring Center. **In Paonia:** Alex Erickson of the Paonia Ranger District. **In the Carbondale and Glenwood Springs areas:** John Almond of the Sopris Ranger District, Gene Hebert and Ken Hause of the Colorado Rocky Mountain School, Bob Morse of Sunlight Ski Area and Clem Lundberg of Chilton's Sporting Goods. **In Eagle:** Bruce Batting of Vail Ski Touring & Guide Service. **In Rifle:** Mike Edrington and Gary Brunk of the Rifle Ranger District. **In the Grand Junction area:** Gerald D. Mayberry of the Collbran Ranger District, Jim Jacobson and Dale Bittle of the Grand Junction Ranger District, Dave Huntley of Marmot Mountain Works, Terry Paulson of Mesa Lakes Resort, and Franz Froelicker of Powderhorn Ski Area.

We extend our appreciation also to Lou Bowlds and Janelle Dykes of the Rocky Mountain Ski Association for their continued support and endorsement of the RMSA Ski Touring Guidebook series. To Horst Klea and Bill Johnson of Fischer of America, Inc., we report our continued enjoyment and satisfaction with our Europa skis ... which now have another 600 miles on them! And to "Butch" Widen of Sportco, Inc., we submit that the ODLO ski touring suits kept us warm, safe and stylish — both in training and touring — throughout our treks into the Rocky Mountains.

All tours in this book were skied by the authors in the 1976-77 ski season. In an effort to make future editions of this book up-to-date and useful, we invite any comment, correction, or suggestion. Please direct correspondence to the authors in care of: COLORADO SKI TOURS, Box 636, Steamboat Springs, Colorado 80477.

LANGLAUFEN LEBEN LANGREN!

T.S.
S.S.

Contents

LEGEND

STARTING POINT   ●

TRAIL   – – – – – –

ALTERNATE ROUTE   – – –→

MILEAGE   **9.0**

AVALANCHE DANGER   ✳

STOPPING POINT   O

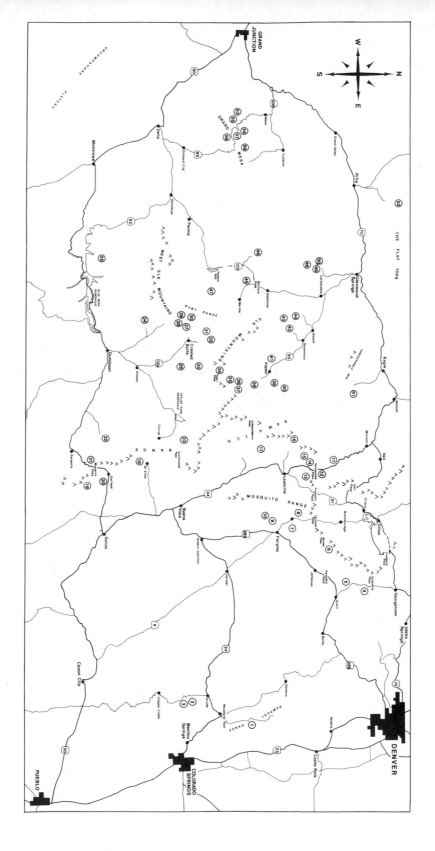

1 SAYLOR PARK

Half-day and one day trips
Terrain: Easiest to more difficult
Distance: 1.5 miles/2.4 KM. one way
Skiing time: 1 hour one way
Elevation loss: 250 feet/76 M.
Maximum elevation: 9,300 feet/2,835 M.
Season: January through mid-March
Topographic maps:
  U.S.G.S. Mount Deception, Colo. 1954
  U.S.G.S. Dakan Mountain, Colo. 1956
Pikes Peak Ranger District
Pike National Forest

Saylor Park, in the Rampart Range north of Woodland Park, claims distinction for being the first designated "Ski Touring Area" in the Pike National Forest, officially opened in the winter of 1970-71. A number of routes of varying difficulty, some but not all marked by sign or letter, lead down onto the open snowfields of the park (see map), and loop tours or cross-country explorations through the surrounding lodgepole pine are easily possible also. The ridge route from point "A" north into the park and the Saylor Park Road from points "B" to "I" to "H" offer the easiest access with the least orienteering problems; "C" and "D" make the best starting points when snow conditions are marginal for an unmarked but easy cross-country trek east to the park; both north approaches, from points "E" to "F" to "G" and to "H", require more skiing and orienteering expertise due to misleading ridges and more cluttered pathways. Except on windy days, Saylor Park itself is the main delight of every tour where everyone from beginners to old pros can race over snowfield after snowfield without interruption, gliding from one end to the other for over 1½ miles one way. For more information and for an area map (without elevation contours), obtain the Saylor Park ski touring brochure from the Pikes Peak Ranger District, 320 W. Fillmore St., Colorado Springs, CO 80907.

Drive northwest from Colorado Springs on U.S. 24 to Woodland Park. Turn right (east) onto the Rampart Range Road access, marked by a sign, turn left (northeast) after two blocks onto Baldwin St., then fork left after another 2.7 miles where the pavement ends and a right fork leads to the "Rampart Reservoir." Follow the Rampart Range Road north past the Monument turnoff and proceed another 4.2 miles to the Ice Cave Creek Road junction, a possible tour starting point (marked "A" on the map). For other starting points, continue up the road, passing point "B", the Saylor Park Road, in 1.8 miles, point "C" in 2.2 miles, point "D" in 2.6 miles, and point "E" in 3.5 miles from the Ice Creek Road junction. Find parking in out-of-the-way spots along the roadside.

For a tour from point "A" at the Ice Cave Creek Road junction to point "H" in the middle of Saylor park as figured in the information capsule, ski up the Ice Cave Creek roadbed for some 150 yards, then turn left into the trees on a cross-country route. Pass an obvious drainage which leads northwest, too cluttered for easy skiing, and climb slightly to the ridge on the left side. Glide north-northwest through the lodgepole pine for 0.4 mile, staying high where gullies drop to the left and right; pick up the southernmost arm of Saylor Park on the left (another good access) and soon begin a quick, fun drop through the conifers to the open snowfields of the park proper. Glide north past a junction of three tributaries at mile 0.6, pass an opening right beneath a prominent rock buttress then another left, all shown on the topo, and continue by an earth dam which marks the pond at 0.9 miles.

Continue north through a wide, willow-filled section, cross more flat snowfields, and come to the Gravel Pit Road at mile 1.5, a discernible scar on the south-facing hillside. From this point, marked "H" on the map, the tour can be continued east to the gravel pit area ("G") then southwest to the trailhead ("A") via the Ice Cave Creek Road. A more difficult extension is possible by skiing north beyond Saylor Park to the narrow East Plum Creek drainage ("F") and climbing northwest along the ridge to the Rampart Range Road ("E"). Or an easy return can be made by turning left onto the Saylor Park Road, climbing slightly and following the near-level roadbed southwest to another meeting with the Rampart Range Road ("B").

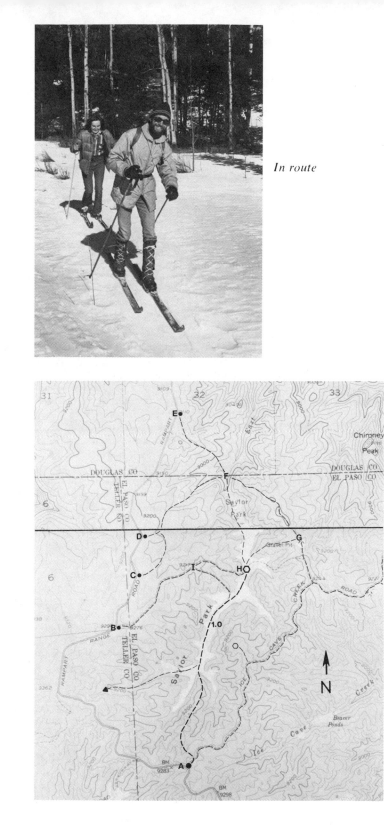

In route

2 THE CRAGS

Half-day trip
Terrain: Easiest to more difficult
Distance: 1.9 miles /3.1 KM. one way
Skiing time: 1-1½ hours one way
Elevation gain: 680 feet/207 M.
Maximum elevation: 10,700 feet/3,261 M.
Season: Mid-December through March
Topographic maps:
  U.S.G.S. Divide, Colo. 1954
  U.S.G.S. Woodland Park, Colo. 1954
  U.S.G.S. Pikes Peak, Colo. 1954
Pikes Peak Ranger District
Pike National Forest

The many-fingered corridors which lead to high, rock pinnacles called The Crags, northwest of the Pikes Peak range, have become one of the most popular places to ski for Colorado Springs residents, due mainly to the easy, 40 minute drive to the area and to the consistently good ski conditions. A main trail, measured for the information capsule and described below, begins at The Crags Campground, climbs gently along Fourmile Creek, then a northerly branch of Fourmile, and ends near the rugged cliffs of The Crags, a perfect lunch spot (if not windy) and lookout point. Other possible routes, often packed out by the crowds of skiers, include the main Fourmile Creek valley from the campground to The Crags, the wide roadbed south from the campground toward Horsethief Park (see No. 3), and the shaded Fourmile Creek valley between the Rocky Mountain Mennonite Camp and the campground.

One annoying problem about The Crags area at this time is the fact that jeeps, unrestricted by a definite point of motor closure on the road, tear up the roadbed and snowpack in an attempt to gain a few more hundred yards of access. For current road conditions, contact the Pikes Peak Ranger District, telephone (303) 636-1602. Use camp stoves instead of fires in this high use area, pack out all litter, and give thoughtful consideration to all of the winter backcountry ethics.

From Colorado Springs drive northwest on U.S. 24 to Woodland Park, then continue southwest for 7.0 miles to Divide. Turn south onto Colo. 67, proceed another 4.4 miles to a road junction, marked by a ''Rocky Mountain Camp'' sign, turn left (east) and drive as far as road conditions permit, usually another 1.7 miles to the Rocky Mountain Mennonite Camp, sometimes to The Crags Campground, 3.2 miles from Colo. 67.

Pick up the trailcut at the east end of The Crags Campground loop, marked ''Trail To The Crags,'' and proceed through several short climbs, staying above the Fourmile creekbed (right). Break onto an open, wind- and ski-packed hillside after 0.4 mile where a Fourmile Creek tributary, used also as a ski route, branches right. Glide easily through scattered aspen and above spruce in the creekbed, bearing toward the 11,476-foot spire cluster which shows through the valley at 46°/ENE and enter a large, willow-filled park at mile 0.6. Continue northeast up either side of the valley where skiing is easiest; bend left across the creek near 1.0 mile in front of a granite block and thick conifer stand and soon come to two branches of Fourmile Creek, both offering ski routes (see map).

Fork left for the main route, wind north-northwest on an easy climb into shady spruce, then begin bending slightly right and break into a shallow basin at 1.7 miles. Continue another 0.2 mile over the open snow-fields to a slight saddle beneath the high rocky pinnacles of The Crags, a good lookout and stopping point. Return over the ski tracks, or if snow cover is adequate, drop east through the rocks into the main drainage of Fourmile Creek, then loop southwest to the main trail.

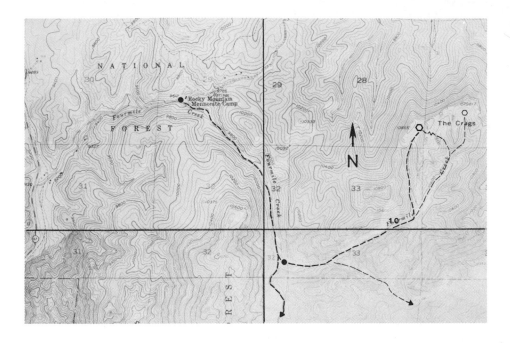

The crags

3 HORSETHIEF PARK

Half-day trip
Terrain: Most difficult
Distance: 1.4 miles/2.3 KM. one way
Skiing time: 1 hour one way
Elevation gain: 580 feet/177 M.
Maximum elevation: 10,260 feet/3,127 M.
Season: Mid-December through March
Topographic maps:
  U.S.G.S. Cripple Creek North, Colo. 1951
  U.S.G.S. Pikes Peak, Colo. 1951
Pikes Peak Ranger District
Pike National Forest

West of Pikes Peak, beneath the high, distinct cone of Sentinel Point, the pines of the Black Forest open slightly to form the secluded, "L"-shaped basin known as Horsethief Park. The Forest Service has established a "ski touring and snowshoeing area" here, closed to motorized vehicles, with a route that first loops over the top of the unique tunnel on Colo. 67 and then climbs steeply for a half-mile to the park opening. Although the rest of the tour route into either the north-south or east-west branch of the park provides delightful, "easiest" skiing, the first steep climb (and fast, difficult return) discourages many beginning skiers, and thus the park receives less use than the nearby, and more gentle, Crags area (No. 2). For a fun extension of the tour, take the north-south branch of Horsethief Park, climb north over the Black Forest range via a wide trailcut (see map), then make a steep drop and stay on the upper Crags Campground Road through private property to the campground.

From Colorado Springs drive northwest on U.S. 24 to Woodland Park, then continue southwest for 7.0 miles to Divide. Turn south onto Colo. 67, proceed past the "Rocky Mountain Camp" turnoff at 4.4 miles, and stay left on Colo. 67 after 5.4 miles where another paved road forks right to Midland. Pass carefully through a one-car tunnel and park along the right side of the road at the tunnel's south end, 3.9 miles from the Midland fork.

Ski north from the parking area into a small gully, climb slightly past a "Ski Touring And Snowshoeing Area" sign, then stay right where a roadbed continues left and climb through a switchback to the ridgetop at 0.1 miles. Cross the top of the road tunnel, begin a steep climb — often with forward sidestep — through a hillside corridor of trees, and break into the bottom of Horsethief Park after 0.7 mile. Rocky, cone-shaped Sentinel Point, in view earlier along the climb, shows now on the horizon at 56°/ENE, and a barren, wind-swept range, not the Pikes Peak range which lies farther east, stretches to the right.

Continue north into the long, open snow-fields which lead toward The Crags Campground, or bear east, as computed in the information capsule, and glide along the right side of the park where the snow holds well. Pass several shallow ravines on the left which make alternate ski routes and bend slightly right into a dead-end gulch at 1.4 miles, a final stopping point for the tour. Return over the ski tracks.

Afternoon glide

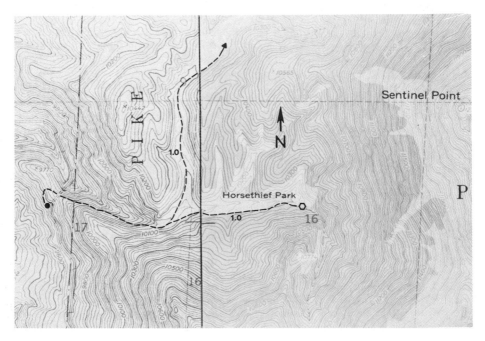

4 GUANELLA PASS AREA

One day trip
Terrain: Easiest through most difficult
Distance: 8.1 miles/13.0 KM. one way
Skiing time: 3½-4 hours one way
Accum. elevation gain: 180 feet/55 M.
Accum. elevation loss: 2,230 feet/680 M.
Maximum elevation: 11,670 feet/3,557 M.
Season: Late December through March
Topographic map:
  U.S.G.S. Mt. Evans, Colo. 1957
South Platte Ranger District
Pike National Forest

When a new snow blankets the Front Range and the whipping wind has yet to rearrange the snow drifts, then conditions for touring on Guanella Pass are at their best. The tours here begin with an impressive vista of a sharp, rocky ridge, aptly called The Sawtooth, and of the massive, 14,060-foot Mt. Bierstadt, named for the famous painter of American landscapes, Albert Bierstadt, whose classic work, "Storm Over The Rockies," depicts nearby Mt. Evans. Rather than following the summer trail, one recommended ski route drops gently into the Scott Gomer Creek basin at the foot of Mt. Bierstadt, makes an exciting but easy descent down the creekbed, and continues via the Rosalie Trail to a slight saddle at mile 2.8, a good turn-around point.

For skiers with competent downhill technique, an all-day tour, as figured for the information capsule, follows the "middle fork" drainage through rolling drops to the three-sided shelter at mile 4.3, then continues through steep, rocky chutes on the Abyss Lake Trail to an end near Burning Bear Campground. Or, if snow conditions are good, the Abyss Lake Trail can be skied up the valley for about 2 miles to the second crossing of Scott Gomer Creek, a superb route for intermediate skiers. Yet another tour route, broken out many times through the winter, bears east from Guanella Pass toward the large amphitheater beneath The

Sawtooth (beware avalanches on the steeper slopes). For a report on snow conditions, check with the Geneva Basin Ski Area, telephone (303) 569-2411.

From Grant on U.S. 285 turn north onto the Guanella Pass Road, marked by a "Georgetown 24" sign. Drive 5.3 miles to a possible starting point or car drop-off at the Abyss Trail parking area, and then proceed another 8.2 miles to the top of Guanella Pass. Or turn south from I. 70 at Georgetown, intercept the Guanella Pass Road at the south end of town, and continue for 10.7 miles to the top of the pass. Park in the large pullout east of the road.

Begin skiing southeast on an easy descent toward the shallow Scott Gomer Creek basin, picking a cross-country course on drifted furrows between the willows. Curve south and glide on or near the level creekbed — sometimes snow-covered, sometimes wind-swept and icy — on a quiet, isolated course between Mt. Bierstadt left and other bare, rolling hills right. Leave the creekbed after 2.3 miles before entering an area of rocky, dangerous ledges: fork left where the creek turns slightly left and a sign reads "Rosalie Trail," etc. and begin a slight climb over the summer trail to a saddle at mile 2.8, marked with the first clumps of spruce on the route. This high point provides a good perspective of the country just passed — the broad flanks of Mt. Bierstadt, the wide, snow-drifted valley, the round hills of the Geneva Mountain range — and also makes a good watching place for snowshoe hare, fox, coyote, and other animals that inhabit these hillsides.

For the "most difficult" extension, drop southwest from the saddle, stay right of the creek bottom and follow new blazes on a fast, 1.5-mile drop to the three-sided shelter. Hike, if necessary, through a steep, rocky drop for several hundred yards to good snow, then pass a new sign reading "Geneva Park," etc., make another steep drop and continue on a gradual grade into aspen and pine. Swing left across a bridge after 5.0 miles, make a long, easy climb through gray-trunked lodgepole pine, and recross the creek at 5.9 miles, an opening which gives view far up the valley to snow-covered summits. Glide over the now-wide roadbed through slight climbs and drops, excellent terrain for ski touring, and eventually break into the open snowfield at the highway, the end point for the tour.

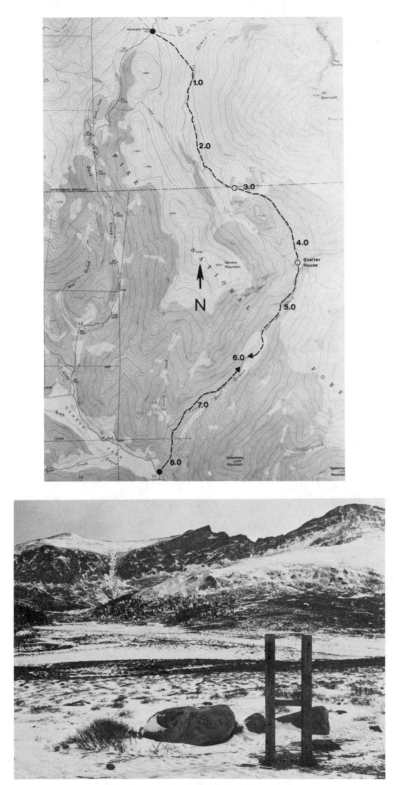

The Sawtooth and Mount Bierstadt

9

5 BURNING BEAR TRAIL

One day trip
Terrain: Easiest through most difficult
Distance: 3.7 miles/6.0 KM. one way
Skiing time: 2½-3½ hours one way
Accum. elevation gain: 1,280 feet/390 M.
Accum. elevation loss: 30 feet/9 M.
Maximum elevation: 10,860 feet/3,310 M.
Season: January through mid-March
Topographic maps:
   U.S.G.S. Mt. Evans, Colo. 1957
   U.S.G.S. Montezuma, Colo. 1958
   U.S.G.S. Jefferson, Colo. 1958
South Platte Ranger District
Pike National Forest

The Burning Bear Trail hugs the shaded, north-facing side of "Burning Bear Mountain" where the snow cover stays longest from storm to storm. Often when wind has stripped Geneva Park and Guanella Pass (No. 4) of snow, this trail will still be skiable. For the most accurate report on local snow conditions, call the Geneva Basin Ski Area, telephone (303) 569-2411. The trail meanders past the snowfields of Geneva Park into Burning Bear Valley and stays on "easiest" terrain as far as the buck fence at 1.8 miles, a nice destination for beginning skiers. If snow depth is adequate, the tour can be continued through "more difficult" terrain to a scenic meadow with the ruins of several log cabins at 2.4 miles, another good lunch and end spot.

Advanced skiers with secure downhill technique can follow the well-marked trailcut to the saddle at 3.7 miles — the point computed for the information capsule — and then either return down their ski tracks or make the lightning-fast descent south through Lamping Creek drainage to Hall Valley. For this last alternative, a pick-up car is needed on the Hall Valley Road (snow closure varies). In spring only, when avalanche danger is low, the Hall Valley and Handcart Gulch roadbeds provide a tour route all the way to 12,096-foot Webster Pass, from which a route then leads north-northwest through the Snake River Valley toward Montezuma (see Webster Pass Trail No. 26 in **Northern Colorado Ski Tours**). This advanced tour of about 10 miles crosses wind-packed snowfields on the Continental Divide and retraces an old "Post Road" built in 1878, connecting two points now reached by over 53 miles of highway.

Drive on U.S. 285 to Grant and turn north onto the Guanella Pass road where a sign reads "Georgetown 24." Proceed another 5.3 miles and park in the Abyss Trail parking area on the right side of the highway.

Cross to the west side of Guanella Pass Road and continue toward the snow fence at the south end of Geneva Park. Ski along Bruno Gulch Creek (left), cross a bridge after 0.3 mile, then enter a fir forest and pick up the obvious Burning Bear Trail. Glide easily over the rolling course, passing views through the trees of the rounded, often wind-swept Kataka Mountain at 50°/ENE and forested ridges beyond Geneva Park at 314°/NNW. Pass through a barbed wire fence and begin bending west at mile 0.6; ski in and out of trees, bearing toward the 11,908-foot extension of Red Cone at 252°/W, and follow the trail under a dark, cool canopy of pine at 1.5 miles. After several hundred yards of long glides, come to a snow-drifted buck fence, a turn-back point for an easy tour.

Climb steadily past the willows in the creek, stay right where a trailcut forks left, then re-cross the creek at 2.0 miles and contour along the south-facing hillside where snow cover is often thin. Break into another open hillside after 2.4 miles — the perfect place for a picnic — where cabin ruins sometimes show above the snow drifts northwest of the trail. Re-enter tall pine and begin a steady climb after 2.7 miles, pass another cabin, then bend sharply left across Burning Bear Creek. Follow blazes and can lids through four switchbacks on a steep climb and continue through juniper and pine seedlings onto the saddle at mile 3.7, a turn-back point for a long day tour.

Snowy woods

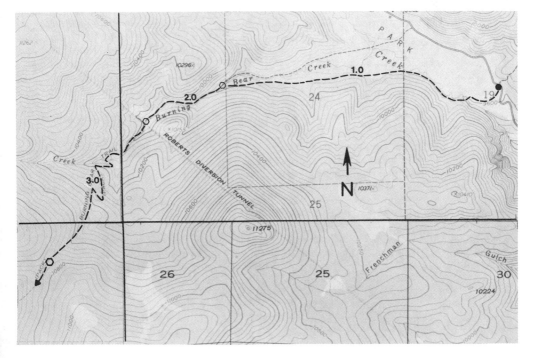

6 MICHIGAN CREEK

One day trip
Terrain: Easiest through most difficult
Distance: 6.9 miles/11.1 KM. one way
Skiing time: 4-5 hours one way
Accum. elevation gain: 1,715 feet/523 M.
Accum. elevation loss: 170 feet/52 M.
Maximum elevation: 11,585 feet/3,531 M.
Season: Late December through March
Topographic maps:
  U.S.G.S. Jefferson, Colo. 1958
  U.S.G.S. Boreas Pass, Colo. 1957
South Park Ranger District
Pike National Forest

Of the five main ski touring areas in the South Park Ranger District (No's. 6-10), the Michigan Creek Valley generally has the longest season with the best snow conditions. Winter storms spill east over the Continental Divide range from French Gulch (a ski route described in *Northern Colorado Ski Tours* No. 33) and snow cover holds well among the aspen and spruce in the wide basin. The tour begins from snow closure on the Michigan Creek roadbed, soon forks right onto a specially-cut trail which shortcuts a wind-blown stretch of road near the Michigan Creek Campground, and then proceeds up the new Michigan Creek Road, drafted onto the map photo and figured for the information capsule. Another excellent ski route, not yet marked but easy to follow, turns right into the narrow French Creek drainage rather than re-join the Michigan Creek Road and heads north across the rolling valley floor to an eventual meeting with the old, steeper Michigan Creek road-cut. Snowmobilers travel the new Michigan Creek Road to some extent, mostly on weekends, and occasionally venture up the other trails. **Note: The upper French Creek Valley is not recommended for touring due to extremely high and unpredictable avalanche potential.** For information on trail changes and avalanche conditions, contact the South Park Ranger District, telephone (303) 836-2404.

Drive on U.S. 285 to Jefferson, 16 miles northwest of Fairplay, 4.5 miles southeast of Kenosha Pass. Turn northwest onto the Michigan Creek Road, marked by a sign, stay left after 2.0 miles where the Jefferson Lake Road turns right, then take the right fork of a

"Y" at 2.9 miles and continue past the 74 Ranch to a designated parking area at a bend in the road, 4.6 miles from Jefferson and about 0.4 mile from the usual point of snow closure. Park here and walk or ski the roadside to the trailhead.

Ski northwest on the Michigan Creek roadbed, passing glimpses of the barren, wind-swept Mosquito Range (seen in magnificent, sweeping panorama on the drive to the parking area), and come to the junction between the old and new Michigan Creek Roads near mile 0.5. Bend left, then fork right from the roadbed after another 200 yards onto a signed trailcut and glide west through stands of aspen and conifers and through open clearings. Drop to the Michigan Creek Road after 1.0 mile, cross the bridge over Michigan Creek, and loop north and west into the French Creek drainage at mile 1.3, the point where two ski routes divide.

For an unmarked, more secluded tour route, usually not traveled by snowmobilers, bear right toward the snow-filled French Creek drainage and glide north-northwest over the historic French Creek Post Road on the right side of the creek. Cross the French creekbed at 1.4 miles, curve west with the drainage, then re-cross the creek at mile 2.2 and climb north around a slight ridge. Stay left around the fenced private property, following a northerly bearing across a basin of willows and conifers. Cross Johnson Creek after 3.2 miles, then continue past Michigan Creek at mile 3.4 and soon intercept the old Michigan Creek Road. Make a steep sidehill climb on the old roadcut, come to the new road at 4.4 miles, and proceed toward Georgia Pass.

For the route on the Michigan Creek Road, proceed south after the French Creek crossing at 1.4 miles, soon loop north and continue past the following landmarks: another crossing over French Creek at 3.2 miles, an easy contour climb to the Johnson Creek crossing, marked by a sign (unnamed on the topo), a loop northeast to the Michigan Creek drainage, and a crossing of Michigan Creek at 5.6 miles. In view here are the shadowed cirques basins of Mt. Guyot northwest and wind-swept hills in the Boreas Range southwest, an expansive and beautiful vista. Proceed the final 1.3 miles to the top at Georgia Pass only if weather and avalanche conditions permit.

Mount Guyot range

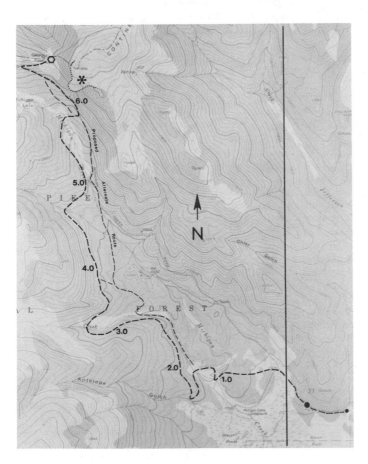

7 BEAVER CREEK

One day trip
Terrain: Easiest
Distance: 3.3 miles/5.3 KM.
Skiing time: 2-2½ hours one way
Elevation gain: 610 feet/186 M.
Maximum elevation: 10,980 feet/3,347 M.
Season: Late December through March
Topographic map:
   U.S.G.S. Alma, Colo. 1970
South Park Ranger District
Pike National Forest

The tour into the wide, willow-filled Beaver Creek Valley starts out from a dizzying elevation of 10,370 feet, representative of the lofty altitudes around all of South Park. High winds and raging blizzards sweep this subalpine desert each winter with a regularity that does justice to the old Western saw: It never snows in South Park but a whole helluva lot blows through! Due to these temperamental weather conditions, the snowpack for this tour, as well as for the Bristlecone Pine Scenic Area (No. 8), Tie Hack Loop Ski Trail (No. 9), and Louie's Loop Ski Trail (No. 10), will vary from snowfall to snowfall and year to year. For best touring, consider these areas after periods of new snow or call the South Park Ranger District at (303) 836-2404 for snow conditions.

Drive on Colo. 9 onto the main street in Fairplay, turn northeast onto 4th Street, then proceed about four blocks and turn left onto Bogue Street. Follow the main road another 2.9 miles into the Beaver Creek Valley and find parking at road closure near the National Forest boundary, marked by a sign.

Follow the snowy Beaver Creek roadbed on a slight curve left to a northerly bearing. Glide easily along willows which fill the creek basin (right), pass turnoffs right and left to proposed loop trails after 0.6 mile (see map), and continue by an open tributary of Beaver Creek (left) at mile 0.9. Stay along treeline as the valley narrows slightly, break to a good view of Mt. Silverheels at 359°/NNE near 1.8 miles and soon pass the Beaver Creek Campground. Begin a slow climb northnorthwest, passing several private cabins, and come to private property at a fence — posted "No Trespassing" — at mile 3.3, a final destination point. Return over the broken track.

7A BEAVER CREEK LONG LOOP (PROPOSED)

Distance: 1.7 miles/2.7 KM. one way
   (to Ridge "10,772")
Skiing time: 1-1½ hours one way
Elevation gain 400 feet/122 M.
Maximum elevation: 10,770 feet/3,283 M.

Two new ski touring trail loops have been proposed — and partially laid out — for the Beaver Creek Valley (see map), routed along old mining roads, gulches and ridges which offer more varied terrain and better snow conditions than the Beaver Creek roadbed. The "long loop", figured as far as 1.7 miles, crosses the valley and climbs the ridge to a splendid lookout of the Mosquito Range. From this point the massive bulk of Mt. Sherman stretches 14,036 feet into the skyline at 233°/WSW and leads right toward Gemini Peak. Horseshoe Mountain with its glacier-carved "horseshoe cirque" appears at 222°/SW and continues left into Sheep Mountain. Looking east from the other side of the ridge, the majestic summit of Mount Silverheels looms closest north, and across South Park the white streak of Kenosha Mountains shows around 54°/ENE and the more ragged Tarryall Mountains around 84°/ESE. Even the hazy triangle of Pikes Peak can be picked out at 107°/ESE to the right of a long forested range.

7B BEAVER CREEK SHORT LOOP (PROPOSED)

Distance 1.7 miles/2.7 KM. round trip
Skiing time: 1 hour round trip
Elevation gain: 250 feet/76 M.
Maximum elevation: 10,620/3,237 M.

The "short loop" makes the perfect tour for Mom and the little kids while Dad and the big kids charge down Beaver Creek Road or ski the "long loop." The tour stays on the roadbed to the first tributary on the left, then loops southwest across a slight saddle and returns on a gentle drop through aspen and spruce to the parking area.

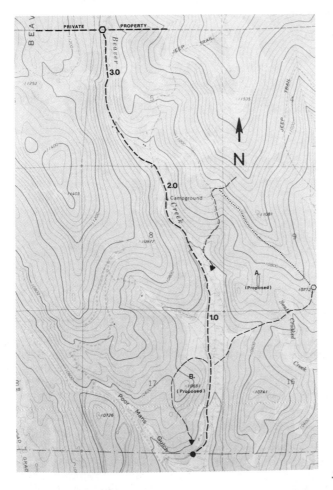

Shadow on wind-crust

8 BRISTLECONE PINE SCENIC AREA

One day trip
Terrain: Easiest through most difficult
Distance: 3.6 miles/5.8 KM. one way
Skiing time: 2½-3½ hours one way
Accum. elevation gain: 700 feet/213 M.
Accum. elevation loss: 40 feet/12 M.
Maximum elevation: 11,720 feet/3,572 M.
Season: Late December through March
Topographic map:
  U.S.G.S. Alma, Colo. 1970
South Park Ranger District
Pike National Forest

The tour to the Bristlecone Pine Scenic Area, also known as the Windy Ridge Tour and the Dolly Varden Gulch Tour, passes some of the earliest mining sites in Colorado and ends on a high ridge among trees whose history encompasses an even earlier — and much longer — period of time. Here are a few historical highlights: Mountain man Joseph Higgenbottom, nicknamed "Buckskin Joe" because of his leather clothes, discovered gold in 1859 in the valley which now bears his name. "Silver Heels," the most beautiful of the dancehall girls (either in Buckskin Joe or Fairplay — accounts differ), became the "Angel of Mercy" when she nursed striken prospectors through a smallpox epidemic in the early '60's. "Snow Shoe Itinerant" Father L. Dyer, Colorado's most famous ski tourer, carried mail in 1864 from Buckskin Joe and Mosquito over 13,186-foot Mosquito Pass to Oro City and Granite (near present-day Leadville), making the dangerous crossing in winter as well as summer. "Father Dyer dropped by Buckskin many a time for a joust with the Devil," states Jerry Davis of the South Park Ranger District. In summing up this route, he adds that the tour "ends with a visit to some trees whose defiance of time and adversity is a little humbling to us mortals."

Drive on Colo. 9 to the town of Alma, 6.2 miles northwest of Fairplay (jct. of Colo. 9 and U.S. 285). Turn west opposite the Post Office and Placer Trading Co. and proceed 2.9 miles to the trailhead at the Bristlecone Pine Scenic Area Road junction, just beyond the Paris Mill. If the road has been plowed only as far as the Paris Mill, use the alternate trailhead, 2.2 miles from Alma (see map). Park carefully along the side of the road.

Begin climbing east-northeast up the snow-covered road to the Bristlecone Pine Scenic Area, soon gaining a good vantage of the Paris Mill and of a high mining shack — part of the Happy Five Mine — on the rocky mountainside at 182°/SSW. Contour beneath an aerial cable from the Paris Mine after mile 0.3. (the first cable shown on the topo has been torn down), begin climbing again and ski by another aerial cable (left) at 0.5 miles. Break into a small clearing after 1.0 mile where the snow is wind-blown and sometimes thin. Continue the climb to a definite ridge at 1.4 miles, then curve left (north) and glide on an easy drop to the basin of Sawmill Creek, a sheltered lunch spot, usually with open water, and a possible turn-back point. Below the trail about 100 yards, an old log cabin can be seen above the drifted snow, a picturesque relic from earlier mining days.

To continue into Dolly Varden Gulch, follow the roadbed on a near-level contour, curving left around the Mt. Bross range. Pass several slight lookouts of icy, willow-filled Mineral Park (below right) after 2.3 miles. Come to a view of old cable towers — one at 322°/NNW — beneath the barren and wind-blown range west, then cross the two drainages of Weber Gulch after 2.6 miles and intercept Dolly Varden Gulch at mile 2.9, the end

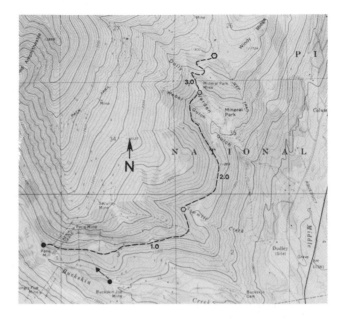

Snowy sign

of the "easiest" route and another good end point. Proceed to Windy Ridge only on days of good weather: pick up a faint road in the middle of the clearing and climb steeply north-northwest up Dolly Varden Gulch. Pass carefully by open pits, mining rubble, an old loading chute, continue by an array of mine shacks and cabins surrounded by large bristlecone pine, then make another short, steep climb and bend right to a sign reading "Dolly Varden Gulch."

Ski east for several hundred yards to a hilltop at 3.2 miles where the view looks down on the town of Alma at 143°/SSE and extends to the white dome of 14,172-foot Mount Bross at 304°/NW. Loop left then right on a steep climb toward Windy Ridge and cross-country northeast into wind-blown snowfields as the roadbed disappears, passing through wind-scarred, low-lying shrubs and large bristlecone pine which have branches only on one side and lean away from the wind. In view also from this open hillside is a wind-swept ridge at 294°/NW that connects Mount Bross with 14,238-foot Mount Cameron. This vista extends right through the rock cliffs of Cameron Amphitheater to another Colorado Fourteener, 14,148-foot Mount Democrat at 278°/WNW. A low saddle of trees marks Hoosier Pass at 6°/NNW and the white snowfields of South Park catch the sun southeast. Return carefully over the ski tracks, using a strong snowplow and pole drag for the first steep drop.

17

9 TIE HACK LOOP SKI TRAIL

One day trip
Terrain: More difficult to most difficult
Distance: 5.5 miles/8.8 KM. round trip
Skiing time: 3-3½ hours round trip
Accum. elevation gain: 850 feet/259 M.
Maximum elevation: 10,750 feet/3,277 M.
Season: January through mid-March
Topographic map:
   U.S.G.S. Fairplay West, Colo. 1960
South Park Ranger District
Pike National Forest

With the opening of Tie Hack Loop and also Louis's Loop (No. 10) for the '77-'78 ski season, the South Park Ranger District joins the Pikes Peak, Holy Cross, and Leadville Districts in offering well-planned and uniformly-signed ski touring trails. This trail, best after new snowstorms, retraces part of the old stage and wagon road that linked the mining camps of Fairplay, Sacramento, and Horseshoe. It was in the late 1870's that the mining activity began in this territory. Prospectors tramped these same woods, "gophering" for pay dirt. Sawyers made cord wood from the pine stands on the south-facing range to burn in the smelter at Horseshoe. And "tie hacks," specialists in the lumberjack trade, cut and hewed railroad ties from these trees for the spur of the old Colorado and Southern Railroad that passed through Horseshoe.

From the junction of U.S. 285 and Colo. 9 south of Fairplay, proceed south on U.S. 285 for 1.3 miles to the Park County 18 road where a sign reads "National Forest Acces/Fourmile Creek Road." Turn right (southwest) and drive another 3.5 miles to a jeep road and gate on the right side of the road. Find roadside parking nearby.

Cross through the open gate of the barbed wire fence and begin skiing at 283°/WNW on or near a jeep road, following blazes from snowdrift to snowdrift. Cross Peart Upper Ditch after 0.2 mile, eventually climb a small hill with a few steps of herringbone, then pass

an old stock pond and cross through a barbed wire fence into a lane of aspen. Come to the end of the loop stem at 0.9 mile after a steady climb up a small basin. For the counterclockwise loop, bend right (east) into open lodgepole pine, and curve slightly left to the ridgetop at 1.1 miles, a possible stopping point for a half-day tour. From here the white summit of Mt. Silverheels, one of the most impressive mountains in the Fairplay area, gleams beyond the trees at 359°/NNE.

Head at 324°/NNW on a fun descent from the ridge, following a well-marked logging road. Cross the tip of a mile-long park at mile 1.3 which gives view to South Park, follow diamond blazes on a winding course through thick, shady pine, and after 1.8 miles come to the south finger of Thompson Park, seen through the trees right. Climb very gradually northwest just inside treeline along Thompson Park, intercept the old Fairplay-Sacramento Stage Road near the upper end at mile 2.7, and turn left on the Horseshoe Road where the Sacramento Road — an adventurous alternate route — continues right. After a rolling climb of another 0.4 mile, turn left from the roadbed and again follow blazes, skiing on a southeasterly course past several open meadows and sinks. Eventually pick up another old logging road, glide south through doghair aspen, then curve east and close the loop at 4.6 miles with a final fast shuss. End the tour by skiing another 0.9 mile southeast over the fast, broken track.

Aspen solitude

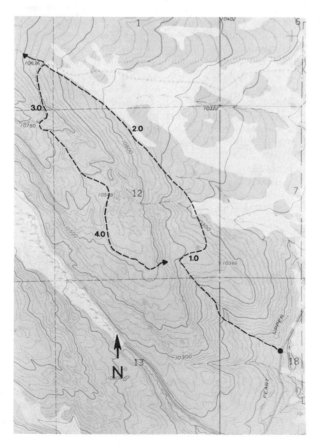

10 LOUIE'S LOOP SKI TRAIL

One day trip
Terrain: More difficult to most difficult
Distance: 5.1 miles/8.2 KM. round trip
Skiing time: 3-3½ hours round trip
Accum. elevation gain: 640 feet/195 M.
Maximum elevation: 10,850 feet/3,307 M.
Season: January through mid-March
Topographic map:
  U.S.G.S. Fairplay West, Colo. 1960
South Park Ranger District
Pike National Forest

Long flats, short climbs, easy rolls and fast shusses combine to make the new Louie's Loop Ski Trail quite an adventure in touring. The route stays near the open basin in Fourmile Creek (well-known among summer mountaineers as the access to Mount Democrat, a Colorado Fourteener at 14,148 feet) for 2.0 miles, then circles back along a scenic ridgetop, passing viewpoints of Mount Silverheels, Mount Bross, Mount Buckskin and other Mosquito Range notables. The final, winding descent from the ridge requires a good snow base to cover the rocks and can be uncomfortably fast, especially when packed. A more gentle, alternate descent, as drafted on the map, is proposed for marking soon. For details and for a report on snow conditions, call the South Park Ranger District, telephone (303) 836-2404.

From the junction of U.S. 285 and Colo. 9 south of Fairplay, proceed south on U.S. 285 for 1.3 miles to the Park County 18 road where a sign reads "National Forest Access Fourmile Creek Road." Turn right (southwest) and drive another 6.7 miles to the trailhead, a point near a Forest Service information sign where the road bends slightly left. Park along the road.

Ski southwest through willows and snowdrifts in the open Fourmile Creek basin, following a roadbed that loops through a proposed campground site. Turn left across an open flat after 0.2 mile and follow another old roadcut (not marked on the topo but drafted onto the map photo). Make a short climb south through aspens to a ridge, contour southeast for several more hundred yards to a trail junction at 0.6 mile, then for the clockwise loop, stay left on a slight drop and continue southeast to the right of the willow-filled basin of Fourmile Park. Glide easily through drifted snow on the northeast-facing mountainside, passing in and out of aspen and occasional bristlecone pine. Bend right through a corridor of willows after 2.0 miles as the roadbed climbs out of the basin, come to a level section and stay right on the ski trail at mile 2.3 where the road continues left.

Link short climbs with rolling flats as the trail winds west and northwest toward the ridgetop. Soon snow-capped peaks begin to flash through openings in the trees: The massive, white mound of Mt. Silverheels shows over 10 miles away at 1°/NNE; a white ribbon of Front Range mountains forms the skyline beyond, highest at 29°/NE near 14,258-foot Mt. Evans. Much closer, the wind-swept bulk of 14,269-foot Mt. Bross comes into view between tree clumps at 334°/WSW, and Loveland Mountain leads toward the tip of Mt. Buckskin at 320°/NNW. Follow trail markers northwest through scattered aspen, pine, and occasional fire-burned snags, turn right after 4.0 miles and make a thrilling drop through several switchbacks to another roadcut. Then drop north-northwest for 200 yards to close the loop at 4.4 miles, and return with a final shuss to the Fourmile Creek basin.

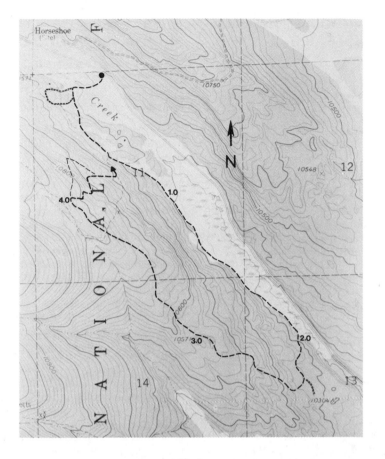

Downhill shuss

11 PANDO AND NO NAME SKI TRAILS

Half-day trips
Season: Late November through early April
Topographic map:
  U.S.G.S. Pando, Colo. 1970
Holy Cross Ranger District
White River National Forest

The Pando and No Name Trails represent two new additions to an expanding system of designated ski touring areas within the Holy Cross Ranger District. Both trails are marked by a trailhead sign with the newly-standardized symbols, colors, and wording (see Introduction for details) and by diamond-shaped blazers along the trail like those used in the Leadville District (No's. 13-17). The No Name Trail climbs very gradually along the unplowed No Name Road for 0.9 mile, then drops south through the bottom of No Name Gulch and returns through a series of exciting but easily managed drops, the highlight of the tour. For an extended trip of over 20 miles, a downhill route can be followed from Tennessee Pass all the way to the No Name Road by skiing the Old Railroad Run to the Wurts Ditch Road, then connecting with the No Name Road above Yoder Gulch (see No. 14). The Pando Trail forks south from the No Name Road after 0.2 mile on an easier course, contours along the forested hillside of the Eagle Valley to a turn-back loop at 1.3 miles — a lookout above the old Pando site — then returns through open snowfields to the roadbed.

Other popular ski touring trails in the Eagle Valley, some marked and others established by use, are described in *Northern Colorado Ski Tours*, including the Tigiwon Road (No. 50), the Lower Gilman Road (No. 51), and the Camp Hale area (No. 52). For more information, contact the Holy Cross Ranger District, Box 0, Minturn, CO 81645.

From the top of Tennessee Pass drive north on U.S. 24 for 8.6 miles to the trailhead at the No Name Road junction. From Minturn drive south on U.S. 24 over Battle Mountain Pass to the trailhead, a total of 11.1 miles from the Ranger Station south of Minturn. Park in the plowed area on the west side of the highway.

11A PANDO LOOP

Terrain: Easiest to more difficult
Distance: 2.3 miles/3.7 KM. roundtrip
Skiing time: 1½-2 hours round trip
Elevation gain: 160 feet/49 M.
Maximum elevation: 9,360 feet/2,853 M.

Follow the No Name roadbed for several hundred yards to a sign reading "Pando Trail/No Name Loop," turn left on the marked trail and contour along the hillside above a large park left. Farther left the sage and aspen knolls in the Eagle Valley can be seen, rising through red, rocky hillsides to white summits on the skyline. Glide in and out of tall, shady lodgepole pine, stay right at mile 0.8 around a knoll where tracks of the return route show left, then swing right (south) onto another easy contour and come to the end of the loop at 1.3 miles. Here the northern end of Eagle Park, also known as the Pando Valley, can be seen through the trees east, crossed by U.S. 24 and the Denver and Rio Grande Railroad. A hundred years ago silver prospectors skied across the flat snowfields of Pando Valley; in 1942 skiers again entered the area when the Army opened Camp Hale as a training center for winter combat. And today skiers glide over the new trails at the south end of the park established by the Holy Cross Ranger District. For the return on the Pando Trail, follow trail markers across the "gravel pit" snowfield to the No Name Road.

11B NO NAME LOOP

Terrain: More difficult
Distance: 1.6 miles/2.6 KM. round trip
Skiing time: 1 hour round trip
Elevation gain: 320 feet/98 M.
Maximum elevation: 9,520 feet/2,902 M.

Follow the No Name Road past turnoffs to the Pando Trail, bend sharply left after 0.7 mile as the hillside steepens, then bend right after another 300 yards and as soon as the road straightens look for a directional arrow left. Cross No Name Gulch, begin a fast descent down the valley, skiing through snow which usually stays soft and powdery, and bend left at a meadow near 1.3 miles to connect with the No Name Road.

Over the bump

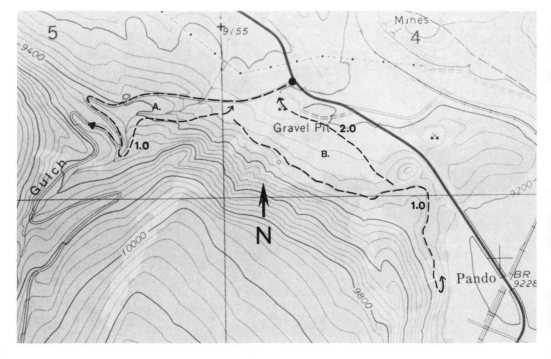

12 TRAIL OF THE TENTH

One day trip
Terrain: Most difficult
Distance: 6.4 miles/10.3 KM. one way
Skiing time: 3½-4½ hours one way
Accum. elevation gain: 1,210 feet/369 M.
Accum. elevation loss: 1,929 feet/588 M.
Maximum elevation: 11,720 feet/3,572 M.
Season: Mid-November through mid-April
Topographic maps:
  U.S.G.S. Leadville North, Colo. 1970
  U.S.G.S. Pando, Colo. 1970
Holy Cross Ranger District
White River National Forest

For advanced ski tourers, the Trail of the Tenth represents the ultimate tour. It begins from Tennessee Pass with an easily-managed warm-up climb up Piney Gulch, crosses Taylor Hill to spectacular viewpoints of central and northern Colorado mountains — Mosquito Range south, Sawatch Range southwest, Flattops northwest, Gore Range north, and Tenmile Range east-northeast — and ends with a thrilling drop down a north-facing, thickly-timbered range. The name of this tour memorializes the men of the U.S. Army's Tenth Mountain Division who trained in these mountains for combat duty in World War II.

Drive on U.S. 24 to the top of Tennessee Pass, following the driving instructions for the Tennessee Pass Trail System (No. 14). Park on the Cooper Hill Ski Area entrance road at the locked gate when the ski area is closed (Mon. through Thur.) or otherwise park in the ski area parking lot. Arrange for a second car pick-up at the South Fork parking area on U.S. 24, 3.2 miles north of Tennessee Pass, 4.6 miles south of Pando.

Ski east on the road to the Cooper Hill Ski Area, then follow the Burton Ditch Road which is marked as the Cooper Loop Ski Trail (No. 13). Turn left from the Cooper Loop after 0.6 mile, cross the Burton Ditch and begin a gradual climb on a 350°/N bearing into the willow basin of Piney Gulch. Follow either side of the gulch, skiing past willows and stumps where snow is best. Bend northeast after 0.9 mile, pass an east branch of Piney Creek at mile 1.5, and continue the steady climb north, gaining better and better views of the smooth, white bank of Chicago Ridge right and the Sawatch Range behind. The white tip of 14,433-foot Mt. Elbert, high-

est point in Colorado, rises above a range of trees at 192°/SSW, the rounded humps of 14,421-foot Mt. Massive, second highest point, dominate the range at 205°/SW, and Galena Mountain, marked with a vast amphitheater, shows at 230°/WSW.

Corkscrew left then right after 1.7 miles as the gulch basin becomes too steep to ski, climb into more open snowfields at 2.0 miles and soon begin a series of long switchbacks up an open, 300-yard-wide basin. Here the vista of the Sawatch Range expands even more, now including the blue-and-white mound of 14,005-foot Huron Peak at 180°/SSW and the Collegiate Peaks farther left. Enter a shady, spruce-and-fir forest atop the "Taylor Hill saddle" near 2.4 miles, turn left (west) out of the trees and follow the snowy ridge toward the top of Taylor Hill. The breath-taking panorama now includes the distant high-point of Mt. Powell at 343°/N in the Gore Range, then a serrated range right to an unnamed 13,015-foot peak at 348°/N in the Eagles Nest Wilderness Area. Snow-capped Ptarmigan Hill at 359°/NNE and Sugarcone Peak at 9°/NNE shape the skyline over six miles away and lead right to the smooth bank of Chicago Ridge. Below these magnificent summits, the Eagle Valley opens into Eagle Park — the Camp Hale site patterned with roads — and leads to the striated Minturn Cliffs.

Curve right along the ridge to the summit of Taylor Hill where a final range comes into view: A flat, white wall of the Tenmile Range rises at 61°/ENE beyond Chicago Ridge; to the left is pointed, 13,998-foot Pacific Peak, to the right are two more sharp, snow-white summits. Begin the ridgeline descent northwest past a steep ravine (right) after 2.9 miles, soon enter thick timber and ski gentle downhills and thrillingly-steep, powder-filled drops. Wind carefully through pine which eventually becomes more open for easier skiing; link openings near the ridge and check the compass often to hold a 320°/NNW bearing. Pass the obvious cut of Upper Jones Gulch Road at 4.2 miles and turn left on Lower Jones Gulch Road (not marked on the topo but drafted onto the map photo) at 4.9 miles. Use a snowplow and pole drag to control speed on the fast, mile-long descent to the South Fork Road (see Camp Hale No. 52 in *Northern Colorado Ski Tours*) and follow the flat course to the parking area at U.S. 24.

24

Tenth trail trek

13 COOPER LOOP SKI TRAIL

One day trip
Terrain: Most difficult
Distance: 6.1 miles / 9.8 KM. round trip
Skiing time: 3½-4 hours round trip
Accum. elevation gain: 1000 feet / 305 M.
Maximum elevation: 11,420 feet / 3,481 M.
Season: Late November through early April
Topographic map:
U.S.G.S. Leadville North, Colo. 1970
Leadville and Holy Cross Ranger Districts
San Isabel and White River National Forests

Cooper Hill on the east side of Tennessee Pass has been the site of a week-end, alpine ski area for many years now. It definitely has the necessary requirements for an excellent ski touring area also. The terrain allows long, easy-gliding contours across snow and spruce hillsides. The view is beautiful, opening occasionally toward the snow-covered peaks of the Sawatch Range southwest and the long, smooth snowbank of Chicago Ridge immediately northeast. And, like the Tennessee Pass Trail System (No. 14) west of the pass, an adequate snowfall usually covers the ground sometime in November and stays late into April, when the season can be extended by skiing on the unbreakable, early-morning crust.

The Cooper Loop Ski Trail, developed by ski-touring Forest Service Interns, follows the concentric contours of Cooper Hill on a well-marked course, with the recommended direction of travel as clockwise. For the beginning skier however, the south end of the loop can be toured counterclockwise with a gentle climb for about a mile, ending in open hillsides with a view across the Tennessee Creek Valley of Mt. Elbert, Mt. Massive, and Homestake Peak. The entire 6.1 miles makes a good day's trip but for the ski tourer who prefers a more leisurely pace and a night of winter camping, a Public Use Tent with cot and pot-bellied stove has been set up at mile 3.0 along a north fork of East Tennessee

Creek. What could be more enjoyable than a long winter's evening in these high reaches of the Mosquito Range, watching the alpenglow disappear slowly from Buckeye Peak (east) and the snowy Sawatch Peaks fill with moonlight?

Drive on U.S. 24 to the top of Tennessee Pass, following the driving instructions for the Tennessee Pass Trail System (No. 14). Park on the Cooper Hill Ski Area entrance road at the locked gate when the ski area is closed (Mon. through Thur.) or otherwise park in the ski area parking lot.

For the clockwise loop, begin skiing from the east end of the ski area parking lot, marked with a sign and a register box. Bear east-northeast on the snow-covered Burton Ditch Road toward the white banks of Chicago Ridge. Stay right on a short climb after 0.6 mile where the Trail of the Tenth (No. 12) forks left across the ditch, and eventually begin a steady climb up the creek basin, a section of fast downhills for skiers on the counterclockwise loop. Pass beneath the alpine ski lift after crossing the creek at mile 1.2, soon recross the creek and make a steep, traversing climb south through scattered pine and picturesque snags, reaching the ridgetop — the Continental Divide — after 2.2 miles. From each open meadow on this last climb the Chicago Ridge gleams on the skyline northeast and eventually the panorama includes the wide Eagle Valley as far as the Minturn Cliffs north-northwest.

Wind east-northeast through conifers along the divide, soon bend right and make an exciting shuss down the East Tennessee Creek drainage to the Public Use Tent at mile 3.0 (location may change in future years). Descend through pleasant dips and rolls left of the creek, skiing through shady spruce and open meadows, and come to the East Tennessee Creek Ski Trail — new for 1977-78 — on East Tennessee Road after 3.7 miles. Contour above the willow-filled basin left and pass through a series of open meadows, giving view around mile 5.0 to a beautiful array of Sawatch Peaks: Homestake Peak at 271°/SSW, Galina Mountain at 242°/WSW, Mt. Massive at 207°/SSW and Mt. Elbert at 192°/SSW. End the tour with a long, easy-gliding contour right — a downhill coast if the track has been set — to a view soon of the towers and green roofs of the Cooper Hill Ski Area.

Public use tent

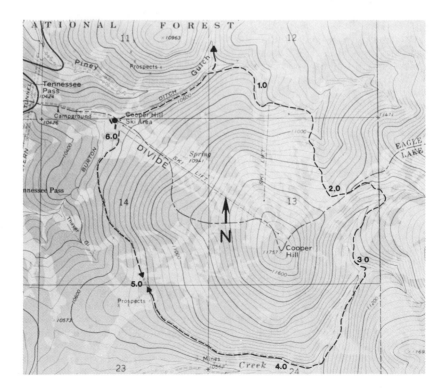

14 TENNESSEE PASS TRAIL SYSTEM

Half-day and one day trips
Season: Mid-November through mid-April
Topographic map:
  U.S.G.S. Leadville North, Colo. 1970
Leadville and Holy Cross Ranger Districts
San Isabel and White River National Forests

The ski touring trail system on the high, snowy summits near Tennessee Pass, developed by Forest Service Interns from Colorado State University like other trails in the Leadville Ranger District (No's. 13-17), may set the standards by which all Forest Service trails are judged. Seven trail segments — all classified, signed, and marked according to the newly adopted procedures for all National Forest lands — combine to form a number of excellent loop tours which offer everything from powder skiing to hardtrack running. Included below are the four most popular trail combinations. Although recently opened, this area shows potential for overuse so be extra careful not to litter, do not use wood fires, and observe wilderness sanitation rules.

In addition to the trail, a Public Use Tent, complete with cot, wood-burning stove, and nearby outhouse, has been set up for day and overnight use, another exciting program initiated first by the Leadville District. Rules: First come, first serve, pack out all litter, leave firewood supply. For more information, obtain the Winter Recreation Program brochure from the Leadville Ranger District, P.O. Box 970, Leadville, CO 80461, telephone (303) 486-0749.

Drive north from Leadville on U.S. 24, turn left on U.S. 24 W. where Colo. 91 proceeds straight to Fremont Pass, and continue another 8.9 miles to the top of Tennessee Pass. Or drive on I. 70 to Dowds Junction and proceed south on U.S. 24, continuing from the Holy Cross Ranger Station in Minturn for 19.6 miles to Tennessee Pass. Either park in the plowed area on the west side of the highway or park along the entrance road to the Cooper Hill Ski Area.

14A TREELINE LOOP

Terrain: More difficult
Distance: 2.5 miles/4.0 KM. round trip
Skiing time: 1½-2 hours round trip
Elevation gain: 280 feet/85 M.
Maximum elevation: 10,660 feet/3,249 M.

From the trailhead sign reading "Treeline Loop" on the west side of Tennessee Pass begin skiing west-southwest up a small hill, following the diamond blazers which mark the Divide Trail. Stay on top of the ridge, maintain a very easy, rolling climb through conifer clumps, eventually make a slight, winding drop and break into a large park at 0.9 mile, a good turn-around point for beginning skiers. Here the surrounding alpine ranges come into view: the distant, pointed peaks of the Gore Range, highest near 13,534-foot Mt. Powell over 26 miles away at 346°/N, the white, pointed summit of Homestake Peak (also seen earlier) at 266°/W, the flat-topped Galina Range with its rugged cirque at 236°/WSW, then farther left, other snow-clad peaks in the Sawatch Range with 14,421-foot Mt. Massive appearing highest at 194°/SSW. Cross the open park, fork left onto the Treeline Trail at 1.1 miles, then drop on a winding traverse for 0.3 mile to the Main Range Trail and contour northwest to the starting point.

14B POWDERHOUND LOOP

Terrain: More difficult
Distance: 2.8 miles/4.5 KM. round trip
Skiing time: 1½-2 hours round trip
Accum. elevation gain: 330 feet/101 M.
Maximum elevation: 10,660 feet/3,249 M.

Ski west-southwest over the Divide Trail on the ridgetop, following the same course as the Treeline Loop. Turn right on the Powderhound Trail at 1.1 miles where the Treeline Trail forks left, make an exciting drop for 0.8 mile through open, north-facing snowfields to the Old Railroad Run trail, then turn right and glide over the near-level roadbed to the starting point.

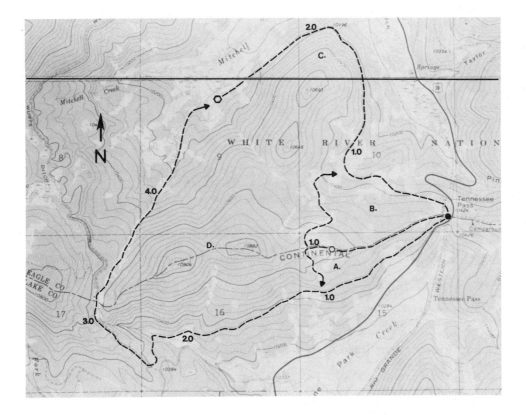

14C OLD RAILROAD RUN

Terrain: Easiest
Distance: 2.8 miles /4.5 KM. one way
Skiing time: 1-1½ hours one way
Elevation loss: 360 feet /110 M.
Maximum elevation: 10,420 feet /3,176 M.

14D MITCHELL CREEK LOOP

Terrain: Most difficult
Distance: 7.6 miles /12.2 KM. round trip
Skiing time: 4-5 hours round trip
Accum. elevation gain: 760 feet /232 M.
Maximum elevation: 10,580 feet /3,225 M.

Turn right at the trailhead sign onto the "Old Railroad Run," a well-marked ski route which follows the historic Denver and Rio Grande narrow gauge railroad bed constructed in 1881. Ski with long glides on a steady, 2.4% descent and come to a slight knoll at mile 0.6 where the ruins of two intriguing kilns stand. From 1887 to 1895 green pine was slowly fired in these beehive-shaped ovens to make charcoal which in turn was used as fuel for ore smelters in Leadville. This knoll also serves as an excellent vista point for Cooper Mountain and the Chicago Ridge east, the deep Eagle Valley as far as the Minturn Cliffs north, and the spectacular peaks in the Sawatch Range, with pointed, 13,209-foot Homestake Peak at 258°/W. Curve left then right through a basin, passing the Powderhound Trail at 0.8 mile. Swing gradually left onto a more shaded trail after 1.5 miles and continue the steady drop southwest until breaking into the Mitchell Creek Valley at mile 2.8, an ending point for an "easiest" tour. Return over the ski tracks on an easy climb.

Begin skiing from the Mitchell Creek Loop trailhead sign on the west side of Tennessee Pass. Follow the blazed Main Range Trail — part of the Colorado Trail (see Introduction) — on a contour west-southwest through tall, shady pine, pass the Treeline Loop turnoff at 1.1 miles, soon ski through a clearing which gives an expansive view of the Sawatch Range and climb and drop to crossings of West Tennessee Creek tributaries. Intercept the snowmobile-packed Wurts Ditch Road at 2.5 miles, proceed northwest then north past the deeply-eroded ditch, then cross the Wurts Ditch bridge at mile 3.1 and fork right onto the Mitchell Creek Trail, closed to snowmobiles. Pass the Public Use Tent on the right of a meadow at 3.4 miles (tent location may change), begin a series of long, thrilling drops, especially fast with packed or crust snow, and after 4.8 miles come to the Old Railroad Run Trail which provides an easy, constant return climb. The railroad grade also loops northeast on a slight drop for 1.6 miles to the old site of Mitchell, an alternate stopping point.

Coke oven

15 LILY LAKE SKI TRAIL

One day trip
Terrain: Easiest
Distance: 2.7 miles/4.3 KM. one way
Skiing time: 2-2½ hours one way
Accum. elevation gain: 485 feet/148 M.
Accum. elevation loss: 75 feet/23 M.
Maximum elevation: 10,590 feet/3,228 M.
Season: Late November through early April
Topographic map:
   U.S.G.S. Leadville North, Colo. 1970
Leadville Ranger District
San Isabel National Forest

The Lily Lake Ski Trail penetrates the West Tennessee Creek Valley to the small, snowy opening of Lily Lake. It is a delightfully easy, rolling course through lodgepole pine and snowy parks, and thus, it makes an excellent selection for families, large groups, and beginning skiers. Signed and blazed with the newly standardized Forest Service symbols, the tour route actually follows the West Tennessee Road which serves as a public access through private property. Besides ski tourers, the snow-covered roadbed provides a course for other winter travelers. On weekends especially, snowmobilers drive the road, usually only as far as the Wurts Ditch Road junction at mile 1.0. Snowshoers also make tracks throughout this area, and occasionally Leadville locals use the roadbed as a training course for their dog sled teams. If you should happen to see this latter spectacle of yapping, lunging Huskies and of yelling, sled-bound driver, it will make a memorable impression in itself.

Drive on U.S. 24 north of Leadville, turn left on U.S. 24 W. where Colo. 91 proceeds straight to Fremont Pass, and then continue another 7.3 miles to the West Tennessee Road junction. From the top of Tennessee Pass, drive south on U.S. 24 for 1.6 miles to this junction. Turn west, proceed another 500 yards to snow closure and park carefully in the plowed area.

Begin skiing west over the wide, level roadbed, often snow-packed by skiers and snowmobilers. Curve slightly right, pass a private home left and a snow gauge right, and then continue the easy, rolling course between a hillside of conifers and the willow-filled Wurts Ditch Creek. (In early winter or in light snow years, this first section could be open for vehicular travel.) Curve left on a steady climb after 0.4 mile, crossing a drainage. Climb steadily through a hairpin curve right, then left, and come to the junction with the Wurts Ditch Road near mile 0.7, marked by a sign. This road, a designated snowmobile route, also provides access to the Main Range Ski Trail in another 0.1 mile and to the Mitchell Loop Ski Trail in 0.6 mile (see Tennessee Pass Trail System No. 14). In view from the trailhead at 280°/WNW and from the openings during this first section is the rocky, 12,853-foot peak northeast of Homestake Peak, marking the high Continental Divide.

Proceed south from the Wurts Ditch Road junction and glide through sun-splashed pine to an opening above West Tennessee Creek at mile 1.0. Swing west up the valley, passing beautiful views of the white-capped Sawatch Range ahead left. Follow the arrows on a sign listing "Lily Lake," etc. at mile 1.3, re-enter the pine on a near-level trail, then begin a contour left around a protruding ridge at 1.7 miles and eventually cross the plank bridge over North Fork Creek at mile 2.2. Pass another road just inside treeline that joins from behind left and soon begin breaking into openings which give view over the trees to the Sawatch Range. After one last, easy climb, break into the large park north of Lily Lake from which the high, unnamed peak northeast of Homestake Peak can again be seen at 288°/WNW. The snowy bed of Lily Lake, a good destination point and a fun area for flat track skiing, opens left after another two hundred yards.

For more ambitious skiers, armed with topo map and bivouac equipment, the tour can easily be extended farther west up the West Tennessee Creek Valley, perhaps to a timberline destination of the northernmost West Tennessee Lake. This trip would add 3.3 miles and 960 feet of elevation gain to the tour. **Be extremely wary of avalanches above timberline on the steep Sawatch Peaks.**

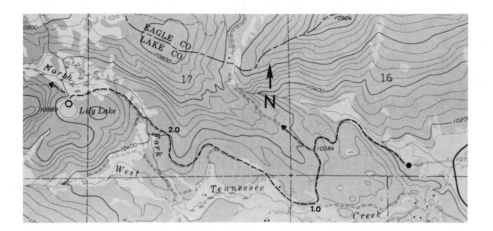

Have a nice day! or Trail graffito

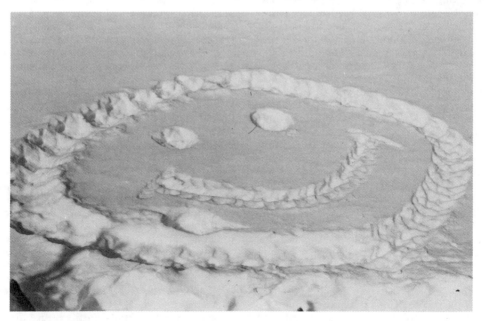

16 TIMBERLINE LAKE SKI TRAIL

One day trip
Terrain: Most difficult
Distance: 2.9 miles/4.7 KM one way
Skiing time: 2-2½ hours one way
Elevation gain: 920 feet/280 M.
Maximum elevation: 10,860 feet/3,310 M.
Season: Late November through early April
Topographic map:
  U.S.G.S. Homestake Reservoir, Colo. 1970
Leadville Ranger District
San Isabel National Forest

The Timberline Lake Ski Trail, marked especially for ski tourers like other trails in the Leadville Ranger District, begins from the west end of Turquoise Lake near Leadville and proceeds northwest up the Lake Fork Valley for 2.9 miles to the snowy Timberline lakebed. Although short, the trip in climbs on a huffing-puffing grade up several hillsides, and the return, with 920 vertical feet to lose, plummets down one drop and then another, providing a fabulous and memorable ride, especially in mid-winter when powder snow blankets the valley. In spring with the fast, sometimes breakable crust or after the trail has been packed out by many skiers, the return descent becomes more difficult and requires a strong snowplow and pole drag in places, challenging even to competent downhillers.

Drive on U.S. 24 to Leadville and proceed through town on Harrison Ave. Turn west onto W. 6th St. where a sign reads "Turquoise Lake Recreation Area 4," soon curve right across the railroad tracks and past the Lake Elementary School, and stay right toward Turquoise Lake after 3.5 miles where the Mt. Massive Golf Course road branches left. Continue another 5.7 miles around the south side of Turquoise Lake to a switchback at the west end, marked "Boustead Tunnel," and park in the plowed area.

Ski past a trailhead sign and register box onto the newly-extended Turquoise Lake Road, not marked on the topo, where another road switchbacks right toward the Boustead Diversion Tunnel. Pass glimpses northwest of the snowy mounds which surround Timberline Lake, glide on the wide, snow-covered road beyond the tunnel construction project north of Lake Fork Creek (scheduled for completion by 1981), then continue under a powerline after 0.5 mile and soon fork left from the roadbed onto a narrower route, well-marked by blazes and an arrow. Cross the Lake Fork Creek, follow the diamond trailblazers on a steady climb through lodgepole pine, and enter a more open hillside near 1.1 miles where the ski trail, marked by a sign, forks left (southwest). The right fork follows the jeep route, usually snow-buried and inconspicuous in winter and used mainly by snowmobilers.

Climb to a high contour along the south side of Lake Creek Valley where the view behind extends to the long, rugged cliffs of Mt. Evans, the middle at 84°/E, and to the rounded, massive Mt. Sheridan and Peerless Mountain Range at 98°/ESE, both over 13 miles away in the Mosquito Range. Ski above snowy meadows nearer the creekbed right, climb gradually through more and more spruce clumps after 1.4 miles, then break out onto a level plateau with a vista of the white-capped, corniced Sawatch Range on the skyline ahead. Re-enter thick, shady spruce on a very pleasant, level contour at mile 1.8, dip across a branch of Lake Fork Creek at 2.1 miles, soon curve around old cabin ruins and hook right across an open clearing toward the jeep road at mile 2.3.

After a switchbacking climb to the roadbed, proceed on a gradual but steady climb through scattered spruce and fir and after 2.6 miles swing sharply right (east) onto a long meadow, a possible stopping point for a slightly less difficult tour with a view of a snow-capped peak at 300°/NW. To continue to Timberline Lake, follow the blazes north back into conifers on one last, steep climb and break onto the wide, wind-swept snowfields of Timberline Lake at mile 2.9, a final stopping point. From midlake the scalloped, rock-studded peaks of the Sawatch Range — the lofty Continental Divide — rise into view west and northwest, creating the proper austere mood for a lake named "Timberline." Control speed carefully on the return drop.

Forest Service interns

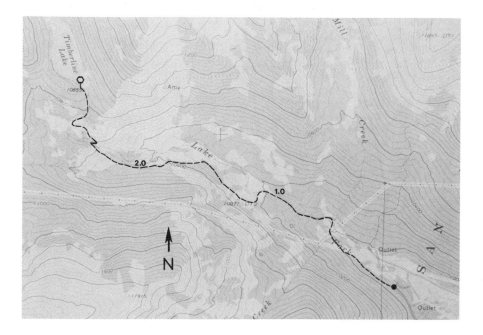

17 HALFMOON SKI TRAIL

One day trip
Terrain: More difficult
Distance: 3.4 miles/5.5 KM. one way
Skiing time: 2½-3 hours one way
Elevation gain: 920 feet/280 M.
Maximum elevation: 10,540 feet/3,213 M.
Season: Late November through early April
Topographic map:
    U.S.G.S. Mount Massive, Colo. 1967
Leadville Ranger District
San Isabel National Forest

The 14,433-foot peak of Mt. Elbert, highest point in Colorado, and the three summits of Mt. Massive, second highest at the north, 14,421-foot summit, make up part of the impressive company for the tour on the Halfmoon Ski Trail. Though these rugged, snow-clad peaks appear formidable indeed, this trail leading toward them follows a level, then gently rolling valley floor and rates almost an "Easiest" classification. Only a few steep sections of herringbone and sidestep near the end of the trail are difficult, hence the compromise classification of "More difficult." As with the other ski trails in the Leadville District, the Halfmoon Ski Trail is signed and marked with standardized Forest Service symbols, and receives exclusive use by ski tourers so it often has an unspoiled, hard-packed track. In addition, a canvas Public Use Tent, furnished with cot, four-plate wood stove, and nearby toilet has been set up at the trail's end, an ideal shelter for bad weather lunch stops and for overnights — first come, first serve. (An experimental program, the location of this tent may change from year to year, depending on use and ecological impact.)

Several good options exist for extended trips. For skiers with accomplished downhill technique, a loop tour can be made by skiing the steep hillside into Halfmoon Creek, and then continuing down a marked snowmobile trail. At Emerald Lake, several hundred yards from the snowmobile trail, a rustic but very comfortable Public Use Cabin is open for overnight use, maintained by Leadville's 10-2 Snowmobile Club (see map). With due regard for avalanche, an extended trip can easily be made from either the Public Use Tent or Cabin farther up the Halfmoon Creek Valley between Mt. Elbert and Mt. Massive. Or the Main Range Trail, immediately above the tent, can be toured north around the eastern reaches of Mt. Massive. Sheltered from wind and most avalanche, this trail — part of the Colorado Trail (see Introduction) — crosses South Willow Creek after 1.5 miles and Willow Creek after 2.1 miles. The trail eventually ends at Tennessee Pass, marked there as a ski trail (No. 14), and thus offers tremendous potential as a major ski touring corridor. Check with the Leadville Ranger District, Box 970, Leadville, CO 80461 for developments.

Drive on U.S. 24 about 3.0 miles southwest of Leadville to Colo. 24, marked by a sign reading "Leadville Fish Hatchery," etc. Proceed west on Colo. 24 for 0.8 mile and turn left onto the gravel Halfmoon Road, also marked by a sign. Continue another 2.6 miles to the first right fork, turn right off the road, and park in the plowed area near the trailhead sign.

The view from the trailhead scans the distant but majestic Mosquito Range, beginning at the 13,781-foot Mosquito Peak at 43°/NE and continuing through Dyer Peak at 60°/ENE, 14,036-foot Mt. Sherman at 66°/E, and Mt. Sheridan at 70°/E down to the southeast. Follow the trail west through stands of fragrant pine, soon bearing toward the rocky top of Mt. Massive. Pass the private Mount Massive Ranch buildings right, bend west-southwest toward the south summit of Mt. Massive, and after 0.9 mile curve south past an open park of willows which gleam with iridescent violet and gray colors. Beyond, all three summits of Mt. Massive can be seen on the skyline.

Break into a larger park at the confluence of Willow and South Willow Creeks at mile 1.5 which gives view to the steep cirque and windswept top of Mt. Elbert at 191°/SSW. Begin slight climbs as the road narrows to a trail at mile 1.7, curve southwest past a large patch of willows in an unnamed tributary right after 3.0 mile and either end the tour at this point or finish with a climb for about 40 yards to the Public Use Tent at mile 3.4, several yards below the Main Range Trail.

Powder plunge

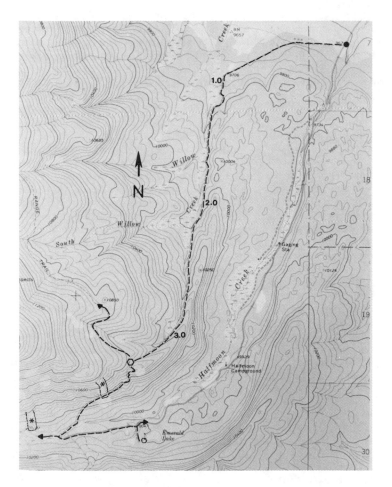

18 SAINT ELMO TO HANCOCK

One day trip
Terrain: Easiest
Distance: 5.4 miles/8.7 KM. one way
Skiing time: 3½-4½ hours one way
Elevation gain: 1,060 feet/323 M.
Maximum elevation: 11,060/3,371 M.
Season: Mid-December through March
Topographic map:
   U.S.G.S. Garfield, Colo. 1940*
     *15 minute series
Salida Ranger District
San Isabel National Forest

Like the Bristlecone Pine Scenic Area tour (No. 8), the trip from Saint Elmo to Hancock follows a high, sometimes wind-swept road-bed, traveling through an area with a colorful mining history. In the early 1880's from 1500 to 2000 people lived in the mining town of Saint Elmo, the eastern terminus for toll roads which wound over the high Continental Divide to the Aspen and Gunnison districts. Prospectors leading strings of jacks passed often down the main street. Wagons of ore, drawn by oxen or mules, returned from the mines on their way to the mill. The Denver, South Park and Pacific Railroad (a name with slight exaggeration) reached the town in 1881 and then penetrated the Continental Divide beyond via 1,845-foot Alpine Tunnel on its way to Gunnison. The Hancock mining camp, located farther up Chalk Creek Valley at a lofty 11,060-foot elevation, once boasted "five stores, one hotel, two sawmills, plenty of saloons and a population of two hundred," according to Muriel Sibell Wolle in *Stampede to Timberline*.

The ski route retraces the old railroad grade, now a fairly wide auto road, and enters the much-diminished Hancock site after 5.4 miles, as figured in the information capsule. Snowmobilers as well as tourers use this route often, mostly on weekends. Other possible tours within the Salida Ranger District — not given a full write-up due to uncertain snow conditions and/or conflicts with snowmobiles — include the Vicksburg and Winfield area via Forest Road 120, the Cottonwood Pass Road from Rainbow Lake (see Taylor Park Area No. 23), the Cottonwood Lake Road, and the well-marked, 18-mile Evans-Rush Memorial Ski Trail. For detailed information on these routes, check with the

Salida Ranger District, Box 219, Salida, CO 81201, telephone (303) 539-2363.

Drive on U.S. 24/285 to the junction of Colo. 162 near Nathrop, 8.1 miles south of Buena Vista. Turn west, proceed for about 9.0 miles to the end of the pavement, then follow the gravel road for another 7.3 miles, continuing through the town of Saint Elmo to roadside parking at the west end. Occasionally the road is plowed only as far as the Mt. Princeton Picnic Ground at the beginning of the gravel road. For road and weather information, call the Highway Department in Salida at (303)-395-2927.

Begin skiing southwest from main street, leaving the picturesque buildings — many restored — of Saint Elmo. Soon switchback left where a barbed wire fence barricades another opening, climb steadily for 300 yards, then switchback right (southwest) where another road contours left along the Mt. Mamma hillside. Pass above a mine shaft and box car, curve slightly left as open parks along Chalk Creek come into view, and continue the steady but easy climb up the valley, gaining a view of the historic, 11,762-foot Williams Pass at 198°/SSW and windblown mounds above the Romley site at 173°/S. Cross through the Romley site after 2.6 miles where the obvious Wildcat Gulch drainage penetrates the range west toward the Continental Divide. Ski by Tunnel Gulch at 4.0 miles which the Denver, South Park and Pacific Railroad followed on its way to the Alpine Tunnel. Eventually bear 140°/SSE toward the snow-covered Sewanee Peak and come to the snow-drifted buildings near the old Hancock mining camp at 5.4 miles. For the return, ski back down the often-packed roadbed, a trip of about one hour.

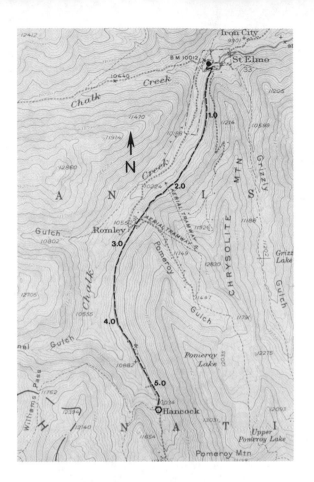

Ice flow obstacle

19 SOUTH FOOSES CREEK TRAIL

One day trip
Terrain: Easiest to more difficult
Distance: 2.7 miles /4.3 KM. one way
Skiing time: 2-2½ hours one way
Accum. elevation gain: 775 feet/236 M.
Accum. elevation loss: 40 feet/12 M.
Maximum elevation: 9,575 feet/2,918 M.
Season: December through early April
Topographic maps:
   U.S.G.S. Poncha Springs, Colo. 1956*
   U.S.G.S. Garfield, Colo. 1940*
    ***15 minutes series**
Salida Ranger District
San Isabel National Forest

When the winter wind scours the snowfields in Monarch Park (No. 20) and spins snow twisters across Old Monarch Pass Road (No. 21), then the protected, secluded valleys of Fooses Creek and South Fooses Creek make a more enjoyable tour route. The trip begins with a hair-raising plummet into the South Arkansas Valley and proceeds on an easy, meandering climb past Fooses Reservoir, reaching the North and South Fooses Creek confluence — a good destination for a short, one-day tour — at 2.7 miles. For a longer trip, the South Fooses Creek Trail provides an enticing pathway, leading south through the aspen- and pine-filled valley along the Pahlone Peak Range. At mile 3.8 a series of beaver ponds fill the creekbed, marking a turn-back point in winter below any major avalanche danger. In spring, after warm weather has stabilized the snowpack, the trip can be extended for another 4 miles to 11,900-foot Fooses Creek saddle atop the Continental Divide. From this point an adventurous "Divide" trail returns northwest past Peel Point and Mount Peck to Monarch Pass, and another trail contours and drops to the Marshall Pass Road south, terrain little seen even in summer.

Drive on U.S. 50 to the junction with the Fooses Creek Road which is unmarked except for a stop sign facing outgoing traffic, about 9.3 miles west from the Colo. 285 junction northwest of Poncha Springs and 3.1 miles east of Ramada Inn at Garfield. Park off the side of U.S. 50 or, if the first descent of

Fooses Creek Road is snowbare, turn west from U.S. 50 and proceed toward snow closure nearer the South Arkansas River.

Ski west down Fooses Creek Road into an open basin around the South Arkansas River. Turn left where a jeep road heads up the valley right, cross a bridge over the river, then ski over a cattle guard and stay on the road through a short section of private property. After crossing a small meadow, pass over a bridge on Fooses Creek, bend left then right around a small knoll, and stay right where another roadbed forks left. Pass under a high voltage line and after a steeper climb of about 20 yards come to the Fooses Reservoir dam, the 0.7 mile mark, where behind, a gray, rubble-filled cirque can be seen on Shavano Peak at 358°/NNE.

Pass through a gate and ski over the level roadbed along the ice-covered reservoir (right). Cross to the northwest side of Fooses Creek at 0.9 mile, continue up the valley beneath the high voltage line, then cross under the line, reenter aspen at 1.4 miles and stay left on the signed trail where another road, unmarked on the topo, forks right. Proceed with long, fun glides over the near-level road, passing fragrant sage and ground juniper then yellow-green pine. Near 2.5 miles enter a small meadow with a few campfire pits, climb at 232°/WSW onto a slight bench, and continue on a narrower road to the North and South Fooses Creek trail junction, marked by a sign. Here the steep-sided South Fooses Creek Valley extends at 158°/S, opening toward a wind-swept knob — fringed with conifers beneath avalanche chutes — on the Continental Divide.

To extend the tour, bear 184°/SSW into the South Fooses Creek Valley, following tree blazes. Cross a footbridge over North Fooses Creek at 2.8 miles, pass the weathered walls of a cabin ruin (right), and continue through conifers then willows. Pick up the South Fooses creekbed (left), now gaining a view behind of Shavano Peak (seen earlier) and 13,657-foot Taylor Mountain marked with switchbacks at 332°/NNW. Cross the creekbed at 3.2 miles, climb steadily along the west side of the valley, and pass beaver-cut willows near 3.6 miles. Continue several hundred more yards into dense trees, pass over a small rise and drop into a large meadow filled with beaver dam at 3.8 miles, a good wintertime stopping point. **Be careful of avalanche danger on trips farther up the valley.**

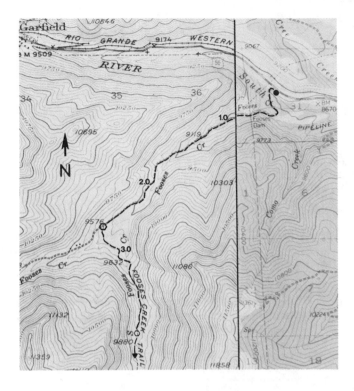

Trail sign

20 MONARCH PARK

Half-day trip
Terrain: Easiest
Distance: 1.1 miles/1.8 KM. one way
Skiing time: ½-1 hour one way
Accum. elevation gain: 100 feet/30 M.
Accum. elevation loss: 50 feet/15 M.
Maximum elevation: 10,475 feet/3,193 M.
Season: Late November through early April
Topographic map:
** U.S.G.S. Garfield, Colo. 1940***
**   *15 minute series**
Salida Ranger District
San Isabel National Forest

The open snowfields of Monarch Park, similar in attraction to the Beaver Creek and Fourmile Park area (No. 50) near Glenwood Springs, make an easily-accessible ski playground for families, beginning skiers . . . and anyone just wanting to poke around a bit on skis. As the old photographs on the opposite page show, skiers are nothing new to the area. Long-time resident of Monarch, George MacKeen, who is now the postmaster and "honorary mayor" in nearby Garfield, remembers well his ski trips in the 1920's. "I trapped marten . . . ran a trap line of 35 traps from Limestone Quarry (Colorado Fuel and Iron property north of Monarch Park) up the valley to what's now the Ski Area," he says, "and I took skis rather than snowshoes because they were faster. From Monarch on, nobody was in that country from November through May. I used a pair of 8-foot skis with a steel plate and leather strap for the toe, and then leather straps for the heel and ankle," George recalls. On skiing technique, he says, "I didn't carry poles, usually. To turn you would use body language. If you felt you were going to fall, you just fell."

When the authors skied the snowfields of Monarch Park in 1977, they were fortunate enough to spot two wild animals: A large, gray coyote crossed the highway near the park turnoff and quickly faded into the surrounding trees, and a less-frightened, white ermine, perfectly camouflaged except for the black tip on his tail, led the authors from snowfield to snowfield while it hunted for moles and mice. Monarch Park maintains this wilderness serenity except on weekends when snowmobilers also use the area. For a unique and enchanting outing, ski the rolling snowfields at night, especially the nights of the full moon in March.

Drive to U.S. 50 to the Monarch Park access road, 1.8 miles south of the Garfield Campground turnoff and 1.2 miles north of the Monarch Ski Area turnoff. No sign except a highway directional arrow and "40 MPH" sign marks the turnoff. Park in the plowed, 5-car parking area at roadside.

Ski south on a gradual, easily-controlled drop on the roadbed, heading toward the white snowfields of Monarch Park below. On the skyline at 158°/S the towers and upper terminus of the aerial tram on Monarch Pass can be seen, and on the forested hillside east white ribbons of roads traverse toward timberline on Monarch Ridge. Cross a drainage after 0.2 mile where ice sometimes spills across the road, then turn slightly left to a crossing of the diminutive South Arkansas River. From the park bottom several routes can be followed for short, half-mile excursions: the main road stays in the basin and heads south on an easy, level course, and the park basin opens north for a tour toward Colorado Fuel and Iron Company's Madonna Mine and the old site of Monarch. Another road forks left from the main road near the middle of Monarch Park and connects with a powerline right-of-way which proceeds toward Monarch Pass. Although this route — and the valley bottom — is skied occasionally from Monarch Pass down to Monarch Park by locals (many trained in avalanche detection), the trip has too great an avalanche risk for general recommendation. **Stay away from the soft-slab or loose snow avalanche paths south of Monarch Park.** For current snow and avalanche conditions, contact the Ski Patrol at the Monarch Ski Area, telephone (303) 539-4060.

Ski tour pioneers

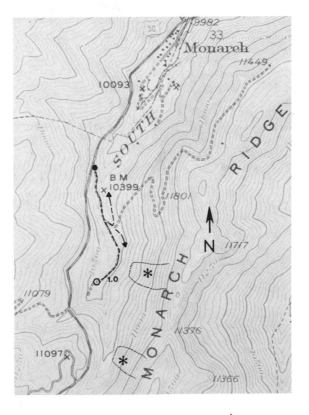

21 OLD MONARCH PASS ROAD

One day trip
Terrain: Easiest
Distance: 10.4 miles/16.7 KM. one way
Skiing time: 4-5 hours one way
Accum. elevation gain: 375 feet/114 M.
Accum. elevation loss: 2,450 feet/747 M.
Maximum elevation: 11,375 feet/3,347 M.
Season: Late November through early April
Topographic map:
  U.S.G.S. Garfield, Colo. 1940*
  ***15 minute series**
Salida and Cebolla Ranger Districts
San Isabel and Gunnison National Forests

"A tour over the Old Monarch Pass Road consists of one good kick with an 8-mile glide," explains Al McClelland of Garfield's Rocky Mountain Expeditions in a bit of ski touring hyperbole. This delightful, winding trek — the most popular in the Monarch Pass area — has a similar elevation profile to the renowned Shrine Pass Road tour near Vail Pass (*Northern Colorado Ski Tours* No. 46). The tour route begins with a fast-gliding climb of 1.5 miles to the 11,375-foot top of Old Monarch Pass, a superb trip in itself highlighted by a distant view of the La Garite Mountains. Then the route descends on an easy, steady 5.2% grade, switchbacking down the ridge between Major Creek (south) and No Name Creek (north) until it intercepts the White Pine Road at 10.4 miles. If the White Pine Road is unplowed, then it provides the exit south, leading to a pick-up point in another mile or two.

Drive on U.S. 50 to the signed "Old Monarch Pass" turnoff, 1.1 miles north of Monarch Pass and 0.7 mile south of the Monarch Ski Area turnoff, and park carefully in the limited space at the entrance to the Old Monarch Pass Road. To drive to the pick-up point, proceed down the south side of Monarch Pass for 8.8 miles to the Gunnison/Saguache

county line, turn right (north) onto the White Pine Road and continue to snow closure, sometimes in another 4.7 miles at the Old Monarch Pass Road junction, more often in another three or four miles.

Begin skiing northwest on a slight climb over the Old Monarch Pass roadbed, a historic route built entirely with horse-drawn Fresnos and slips (graders and sleds) and hand labor in the early '20's. Curve left then right, skiing next to a power line; curve left again to a view of the "new" Monarch Pass with lift towers and a gondola building at 129°/SE and pass glimpses of the top runs of the Monarch Ski Area (right). Climb slowly past a wide basin with scattered trees which drops left (northeast) — **not recommended as a ski route due to 300 yards of dangerous avalanche sluffs nearer U.S. 50** — and reach the top of Old Monarch Pass at 1.5 miles. Sharp, steep-sided Sawatch Peaks loom high into the skyline from this vantage, beginning with Mt. Aetna at 355°/N through cirque-marked Taylor Mountain and pointed Missouri Hill to Lost Mountain at 20°/NNE. And on the horizon southwest the La Garita Mountains, like a wavy, white ribbon, stand out from the forested knobs and hills over 47 miles away, highest near 14,014-foot San Luis Peak at 208°/SW.

Bend right and proceed on a mile-long, downhill traverse past Porphyry Creek (left). Curve left around the forested Major Creek Valley, then switchback left at 3.2 miles and right at 3.5 miles and continue the easy drop southwest along Major Creek (left). Pass scenic, sometimes wind-scoured rock outcroppings along the road and contour onto the north-facing side of the ridge at 5.0 miles where the view soon extends west through No Name Valley. A few white snowfields cap the forested Lake Hill Range at 338°/N, a pointed, distant-blue peak — also in view from the pass — rises conspicuously on the horizon at 230°/WSW, perhaps 14,309-foot Uncompahgre Peak in the Uncompahgre Primitive Area, and the tour stopping point in the open Tomichi Creek Valley shows at 222°/SW. Pass under a powerline, proceed through four long switchbacks, then maintain the gradual drop west and southwest to the 8.0 mile mark. Drop through four more switchbacks and break from conifers to aspens near the White Pine Road. End the tour by skiing south over the White Pine roadbed to the plowed road.

End of the tour finale

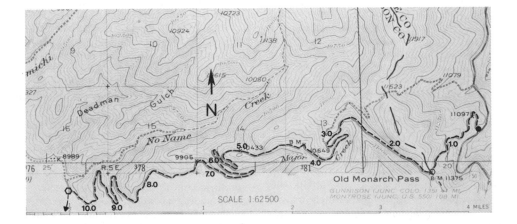

22 HICKS GULCH AND STRIDIRON CREEK

One day trip or overnight
Terrain: Most difficult
Distance: 9.5 miles/15.3 KM. round trip
Skiing time: 5-6 hours round trip
Accum. elevation gain: 1,345 feet/410 M.
Maximum elevation: 10,225 feet/3,117 M.
Season: December through March
Topographic maps:
  U.S.G.S. Pitkin, Colo. 1964
  U.S.G.S. Garfield, Colo. 1940*
    ***15 minute series**
Cebolla Ranger District
Gunnison National Forest

A maze of old logging roads, jeep roads and summer hiking trails criss-cross the pine-covered mountains north of Waunita Park, creating miles upon miles of tour possibilities. The Hicks Gulch and Stridiron Creek loop — also known as the Waunita Hot Springs Trail due to its start near the steaming waters of the Waunita Hot Springs Guest Ranch — was first researched by Western State College students in the Winter Ecology program. At present the course needs better marking or mapping to reduce the orienteering problems. Examine carefully the map on the opposite page for these general features: the Hicks Gulch Road above and left of Hicks Gulch, the steady (and very scenic) climb north and east on the ridgetop, the contouring drop into Stridiron Creek Valley and the return descent via Stridiron Road. The 7.5-minute advance proof of this area, replacing the badly out-of-date Garfield topo, will be available in Stage 6 by October 1978.

Drive on U.S. 50 east of Gunnison to the turnoff marked "Waunita Hot Springs/Pitkin," 7.1 miles southeast of Parlin and 0.7 miles northwest of the Doyleville turnoff. Turn northeast and proceed 8.3 miles on the Hot Springs Road to snow closure at Waunita Hot Springs Ranch. Park carefully in the turn-around beyond the guest ranch, making sure not to block access into the private drive.

Ski east from the Waunita Hot Springs Ranch, following the rolling, unplowed road through Waunita Park. Pass a road which leads left to Pitkin at 0.5 mile, proceed ahead after 0.8 mile where the Black Sage Pass Road — the ski route to the Old Monarch Pass Road (No. 21) — angles right, and turn left (north) near 1.0 mile where a sign reads "Stridiron Creek 1½/Hicks Gulch ½." Continue the rolling drops and climbs to the fork between Hicks Gulch and Stridiron Creek Roads — the end of the loop stem — at mile 1.5. For the counter-clockwise loop, fork right and climb gradually up a sage and aspen basin, gaining a good perspective of the rounded, forested Tomichi Dome at 206°/SW. Begin a steeper climb to the top of a ridge and bend right through a clear cut at 3.0 miles which brings into view the large, distant-blue summit of 14,309-foot Uncompahgre Peak at 223°/WSW, highest of the Uncompahgre Wilderness Area mountains about 63 miles away.

Soon bend left above the deep branch of Hicks Gulch (right) and come to a tri-junction near 3.4 miles. Here the left fork follows a short logging cut, the middle fork climbs steeply for 25 yards on a bend left, and the right fork contours east then north around the knoll, leading eventually to Canyon Creek. On the middle fork, soon stay right rather than take another logging spur left and climb

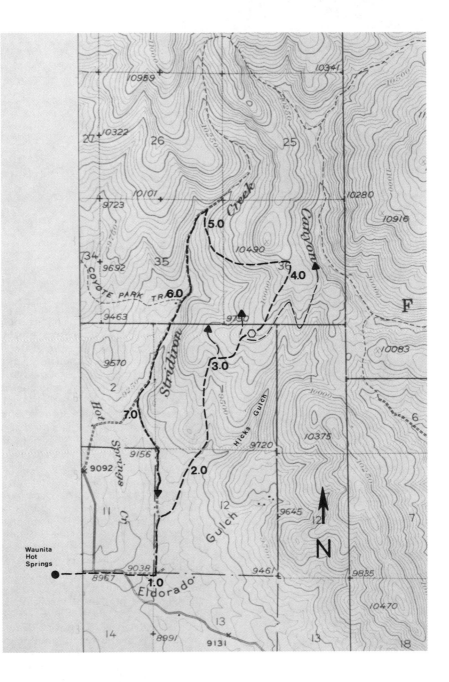

Aspen scene

steeply then more gradually through seedling
pine along the ridgetop. From this high vantage — a nice destination for a shorter tour —
twin, white peaks, rise beyond the forested
range, appearing like giant fox ears, with a
mid-point at 102°/ESE. Follow the ridge at
3.7 miles where a logging road contours left,
ski through scattered seedlings and black,
fire-burned snags, then drop 25 yards from
the ridge and come to a junction at mile 4.1
where two signs read "Stridiron Creek 1,"
and "Buffalo Fork 2/Hicks Gulch 2."

Swing left on an easy drop toward a prominent gulch, soon take a middle fork (which
joins with the left) where a right fork climbs
the hillside, and traverse the hillside south
and west of the "10,490" summit on a fun
drop into the Stridiron Creek Valley. Cross
the creek at 5.2 miles and follow the Stridiron
Creek Road southwest, passing "corral
gulch" which opens right (northwest) after
mile 5.3. Continue into a basin of willows,
pass another prominent gulch and obvious
roadbed which heads left (east) after 5.9
miles, and cross Stridiron Creek. Pass
through a barbed wire fence and re-cross the
creek near 6.0 miles. Continue through easy
flats and gentle downhills on a curve to a
southerly bearing, then close the loop at the
Hicks Gulch Road junction near 8.0 miles,
and return over the broken trail to the parking
area.

23 TAYLOR PARK AREA

One day trips or overnights
Terrain: Easiest to more difficult
Season: Late November through early April
Topographic maps:
   U.S.G.S. Taylor Park Reservoir, Colo. 1967
   U.S.G.S. Matchless Mountain, Colo. 1967
   U.S.G.S. Mt. Harvard, Colo. 1955*
     ***15 minute series**
Map photo:
   Gunnison National Forest Recreation Map
Taylor River Ranger District
Gunnison National Forest

Points of interest on the Taylor Park area: The immense basin of snowfields and sage rises, shaped as a triangle with each side 4 or 5 miles long, fans northeast from Taylor Canyon toward the spectacular Collegiate Peaks in the Sawatch Range. The lowest temperature ever recorded in Colorado was in Taylor Park on February 1, 1951: a chilling -60°F/ -51°C! Taylor Park, Taylor River and Canyon, and Taylor Lake, Pass, and Peak (these last three near the Barnard Hut tour No. 36) are named for Jim Taylor who first prospected the area in 1860. Taylor Park Reservoir sprawls over half of Taylor Park and holds over 2,000 surface acres of water. But the Reservoir and Dam memorialize a different Taylor, U.S. Representative Edward T. Taylor who served this district of Colorado from 1909 to 1941.

In the late 1870's thousands of prospectors stampeded into the Taylor Park area to look for gold and silver. They crossed the Sawatch Range — the high Continental Divide — through several routes: west from Buena Vista through Cottonwood Pass, west from St. Elmo through Tin Cup Pass (see St. Elmo No. 18), and south from Monarch then west over Monarch Pass (see Old Monarch Pass Road No. 21). By 1882 the population of Tin Cup had swelled to 6,000. The Denver and South Park Railroad then provided transport over the range from Hancock via the Alpine Tunnel, the highest (11,524 feet) and most

expensive ($242,000) narrow gauge tunnel of its day. The Dorchester mining camp, northeast of Italian Mountain and Cement Creek (see Walrod Gulch No. 26), came into prominence in 1900 when gold mines in the Italian Mountain District were opened. In winter miners formed the Italian Mountain Snowshoe Club and spent spare hours skiing "the beautiful," as the snow was called.

Thus, Taylor Park and the surrounding valleys offer — to the ski tourer — a vast and trackless territory to explore, with expeditionary routes leading to Crested Butte, Ashcroft, Buena Vista, and Monarch Pass. Described below are two one-day trips, each beginning with an extraordinary view of the majestic, rock-ribbed Collegiate Peaks.

Drive north from Gunnison on Colo. 135 for about 10 miles to the Taylor River Road at Almont. Turn right (east), stay right after 7.1 miles at the Spring Creek Road junction, and come to the "Trail No. 428" junction after another 10.0 miles, a possible starting or pick-up point for the Union Park tour. Proceed another 3.4 miles where a road forks left to Taylor Park Reservoir maintenance buildings and the Taylor River Road heads right across the Taylor River, a point of possible road closure. If the Taylor River Road is open, continue another 3.2 miles to the Union Park turnoff, another 3.5 miles to the Taylor Park Trading Post for the Cottonwood Pass Road turnoff.

Spring camp

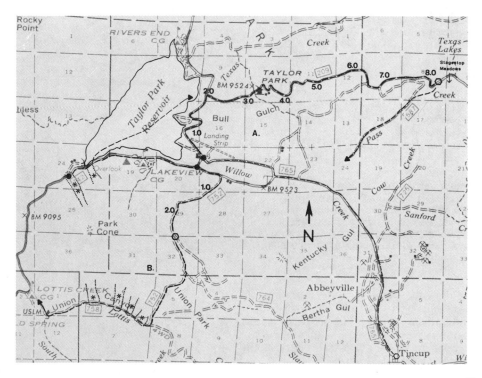

23A STAGESTOP MEADOWS

Distance: 8.2 miles/13.2 KM. one way
   (from Taylor Park Trading Post)
Skiing Time: 5-6 hours one way
Accum. elevation gain: 1,120 feet/341 M.
Accum. elevation loss: 60 feet/18 M.
Maximum elevation: 10,400 feet/3,170 M.

Pick up the Cottonwood Pass Road on the east side of Taylor Park Reservoir, either following a 47°/ENE bearing across the flat reservoir bed or if the road is open, driving to snow closure, and climb east into stands of lodgepole pine. Turn right from the roadbed at ''Stagestop Meadows'' and return down the Pass Creek drainage.

23B UNION PARK

Distance: 2.6 miles/4.2 KM. one way
   (from turnoff south of Trading Post)
Skiing time: 2-2½ hours one way
Accum. elevation gain: 695 feet/212 M.
Accum. elevation loss: 200 feet/61 M.
Maximum elevation: 10,075 feet/3,071 M.

Follow the Union Park Road south on an easy climb to the two-mile-long snowfields of Union Park. Union Canyon/Lottis Creek open west from the southwest corner of the park and provide an alternate return, **safe only when avalanche danger is very low.**

Stagestop Meadows

24 MILL CREEK SKI TRAIL

One day trip
Terrain: More difficult
Distance: 6.8 miles/10.9 KM. round trip
Skiing time: 3½-4 hours round trip
Accum. elevation gain: 760 feet/232 M.
Maximum elevation: 9,140 feet/2,786 M.
Season: December through March
Topographic map:
  U.S.G.S. Squirrel Creek, Colo. 1965
Taylor River Ranger District
Gunnison National Forest

Like the Hicks Gulch and Stridiron Creek tour (No. 22), the Mill Creek Ski Trail northwest of Gunnison is being studied by Western State College students enrolled in the Winter Ecology program. Student teams gather information on snow depth, note the local vegetation and wildlife, and determine a difficulty rating for the trail. Due to this attention and to the generally excellent skiing conditions in the Mill Creek Valley anyway, this trail has become one of the most popular ski tours in the Gunnison area, usually broken with a fast, packed track after each winter snowstorm.

Beginning skiers and families or groups of mixed abilities can ski the first, easy section of the roadbed — the stem of the tour loop — with a turn-back point perhaps after 1.4 miles at the Lone Pine Gulch Road junction. For more advanced skiers, a delightful loop tour can be made, easier in the counter-clockwise direction where the steep hills are managed with a climb rather than a drop. This route, described below, continues west over the up-and-down Mill Creek roadbed and soon enters stands of dense, mature aspen, many two- and three-trunked decorated with black knots, and indeed the most scenic part of the tour. Several alternate routes fork left from the roadbed, making the loop smaller or

larger (see map), and connect with the Eilebrecht Ditch Road which then loops east on a shaded, near-level course to Cunningham Reservoir. From a point at mid-reservoir the tour turns north onto another roadbed and makes a final, thrilling drop to close the loop at the Mill Creek Road.

Drive on U.S. 50 to Gunnison, turn north onto Colo. 135 and proceed 3.5 miles to the Ohio Creek Road junction, marked by a sign. Turn left (north), continue another 9.1 miles to the signed Mill Creek Road/No. 727, turn left again and follow the dirt road to snow closure, usually near the second cattle guard after 1.8 miles. Park carefully in the turn-around area.

Cross over the cattle guard and ski west-southwest over the Mill Creek roadbed where the view extends ahead to conspicuous rock cliffs at 244°/WSW above the Mill Creek Valley, and then to distant, open hillsides, ridges, and ravines north. Stay left through a metal gate after 1.2 miles and make a gradual climb then short drop beyond a clump of alders to a junction with the Little Mill Creek summer trail and the Lone Pine Gulch Road at mile 1.4, the point where the loop closes. Stay right on the Mill Creek Road for the easier route, begin a series of steep climbs for the next several hundred yards, skiing through scenic aspen clumps, then come to the signed North Beaver Creek turnoff after 1.8 miles which leads left on a very steep but possible route to the Eilebrecht Ditch. Climb gradually through thick, beautiful aspen, pass another turnoff left through an open draw at 2.2 miles, then continuing on the roadbed, break into a large park at mile 2.6, marked with a sign reading "Mill Castle Trail," etc., where private buildings can be seen ahead.

Turn left from the roadbed just past the aspen grove on the right, bear 197°/SSW up the open hillside toward clumps of seedling spruce, now leaving the beautiful vista of the Mill Creek cliffs, and climb steadily to the Eilebrecht Ditch Road at 2.8 miles. Turn left again and contour on a shaded, near-level course, passing turnoffs at miles 3.3, 3.6 and 3.9. Loop south then northeast through the sunny Little Mill Creek basin, stay along the left side of Cunningham Reservoir to the mid-point at 4.7 miles, then drop north with switchbacks or telemark turns to the Lone Pine Gulch Road and the Mill Creek Road at mile 5.4 and end the tour by skiing east back to the parking area.

Mill Creek cliffs

Pine tree limbo

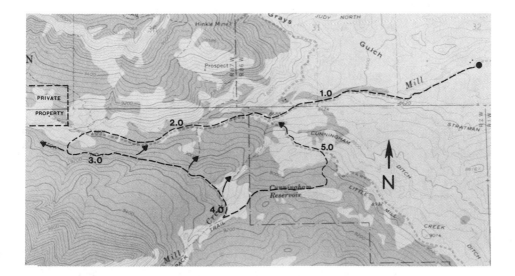

25 CURECANTI CREEK

Half-day through overnight trips
Terrain: Easiest to more difficult
Distance: 2.7 miles/4.3 KM. one way
Skiing time: 1½-2 hours one way
Accum. elevation gain: 320 feet/98 M.
Accum. elevation loss: 40 feet/12 M.
Maximum elevation: 8,180 feet/2,493 M.
Season: Mid-December through early April
Topographic maps:
  U.S.G.S. Curecanti Needle, Colo. 1956
  U.S.G.S. X Lazy F Ranch, Colo. 1957
  U.S.G.S. Little Soap Park, Colo. 1954
Paonia Ranger District
Gunnison National Forest

Far from the beaten path, lonely and isolated, the Curecanti Creek Valley north of the Black Canyon of the Gunnison sees few winter travelers, giving it a special appeal to the adventurous ski tourer or winter camper in search of untracked terrain. Even the drive to the trailhead is an adventure, especially at sunrise and sunset when deep shadows reinforce the vastness of the land. The Colorado 92 highway snakes for miles along the canyon walls and through the scrub oak thickets, dropping gradually east from the Black Mesa, crossing the Blue Mesa Dam and climbing west above the awesome chasm of the Black Canyon. The highway is currently not maintained from 6 p.m. to 6 a.m. and receives little use during those times so take due precautions during stormy weather.

According to Charles A. Page in *What's In A Name?*, Curecanti Creek was named after Curicata, a Tabeguache Ute Chief. The tour route begins several miles north of the Black Canyon where the highway switchbacks through the deep Curecanti Valley, a starting point at a low, 7,900-foot elevation but with a surprising amount of snow. The route follows a roadbed north through private property for the first mile and maintains an easy, rolling course past sage and willows to the Mill Creek Trail junction, the one-day destination computed for the information capsule. Here the valley narrows and beautiful, wind-eroded rock outcroppings begin to show from out of the forested mountainsides left and right, a scenic attraction which continues for miles up the valley. For an extended trip with four or five nights of winter camping — the best way to explore the Curecanti Valley — follow the creekbed north toward a first-day destination near the Trail Creek or Dry Fork Creek tributaries, then penetrate the valley north-northeast past turnoffs to East Creek, Bald Mountain Reservoir, and Sink Creek and drop over Curecanti Pass into the headwaters of Coal Creek for the second night. Pick up the Minnesota Pass Trail beyond Coal Basin, climb past the Three Knobs into the Willow Creek Valley, a third night destination, then cross the Chain Mountains through Minnesota Pass, possibly for the fourth night. Intercept the Lone Cabin Trail/Forest Service 519 and proceed northwest to a car pick-up at road closure outside of Paonia. This challenging trip measures about 40 miles one way and requires advanced skiing and orienteering skills, done easiest with large groups to share the job of breaking trail.

Drive on Colo. 92 to the Curecanti Creek Road west of Blue Mesa Reservoir near the sign reading "Curecanti Creek," about 8.6 miles east of the Gunnison/Montrose county line. Park along the side of the road.

Cross through the open gate of the barbed wire fence and ski up the roadbed along the right side of Curecanti Creek, passing a corral and buildings left. Bend left then right on a slight drop, ski along a fence near the creekbed left, then pass a ranch house at mile 1.1 and continue with slight climbs and drops past the Gunnison National Forest boundary and an A-frame cabin. Contour along the sage-covered hillside, passing views of snow-dusted rock blades and needles on the mountainside right. Ski by clumps of russet and gold willows in the creek basin left which add a contrast of color to the otherwise gray and white landscape; pass more and more spruce along the roadbed after 1.8 miles, and come to the deep Mill Creek Valley, bordered by scenic, rocky hillsides, near 2.7 miles, a turnback point for a short, one-day tour.

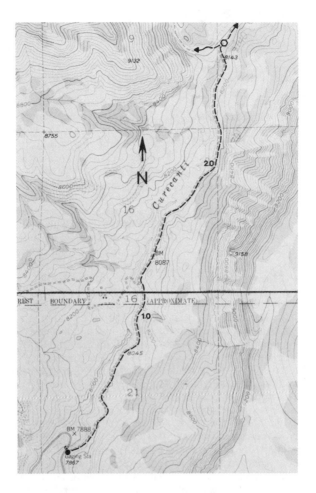

Overnight preparations

26 WALROD GULCH

Half-day or one day trip
Terrain: More difficult
Distance: 3.0 miles/4.8 KM. one way
Skiing time: 2½-3 hours one way
Accum. elevation gain: 460 feet/140 M.
Accum. elevation loss: 840 feet/256 M.
Maximum elevation: 9,740 feet/2,969 M.
Season: December through March
Topographic map:
U.S.G.S. Cement Mtn., Colo. 1961
Taylor River Ranger District
Gunnison National Forest

The popular loop tour through Walrod Gulch follows an all-uphill, then all-downhill course. The climb consists of a series of cross-country switchbacks through aspen and ends at a ridge and lookout, a delightful spot where lunch can be enjoyed with a view of the Cement Creek Valley, Horse Basin, and Cement Mountain. And the downhill through Walrod Gulch, a special highlight of the tour, combines moderate drops with wide-open run-outs, terrain which beginners can handle with confidence. Either end the tour with a car pick-up at the bottom of Walrod Gulch or complete the loop by skiing along Cement Creek Road to the parking area, an additional distance of 1.8 miles and 380 feet elevation gain. **Note the three areas of avalanche marked on the map photo: never ski this route during high avalanche conditions and always observe avalanche precautions while crossing beneath these avalanche run-outs.**

Other good tour possibilities in the Cement Creek Valley include the Cement Creek roadbed for two miles beyond snow closure, an ideal first-timer's route (watch out for avalanche danger after about four miles on the Cement Creek Road), and the advanced, overnight tour into Horse Basin (correctly placed on the map photo), Deadman Gulch, and Rosebud Gulch via the Horse Basin Creek Trail.

In intriguing points of history, Cement Creek, according to Charles A. Page in *What's In A Name?*, took its name from the mountain or valley walls ''for the conglomerate outcroppings, looking like poorly

poured concrete.'' Page also reports that Italian Mountain, seen from the trailhead at the valley's end, was ''named by Italian miners who said the mountain reminded them of their flag of green, red and white colors.'' And for ski history buffs, it is interesting to learn that the Pioneer Ski Area operated about 0.7 mile west of Walrod Gulch in the Cement Creek Valley from 1937 to 1953 and claimed distinction for having Colorado's first chairlift.

From Crested Butte (jct. with Elk Avenue) drive southeast on Colo. 135 for 6.8 miles to the Cement Creek Road, marked by a sign. Or drive north from Gunnison on Colo. 135 to this junction. Turn east and proceed another 3.0 miles to a junction with the Walrod Gulch Road, a possible stopping point for the tour and car dropoff (see map photo). Then continue up the Cement Creek Road to snow closure which is usually in another 1.9 miles, just beyond the Cement Creek Ranch. Park carefully in the limited spaces on the side of the road, making sure not to block other cars.

Ski up the Cement Creek Road for 0.4 mile past the Cement Creek Ranch cabins, heading toward the snow-capped Italian Mountain range which blocks the valley at 9°/NNE. Turn left from the roadbed just beyond the third cluster of aspen, make a switchback or two to a faint horse trail, then swing left and climb to an open saddle at mile 0.7. Do not drop southwest into the drainage beyond which is too cluttered for skiing but bear northwest across the basin and into a hillside of aspen. Keep the drainage on the right and continue northwest on an easy, switchbacking climb through more aspen, gaining the ridgetop after about 1.3 miles. From the ''lunch tree'' here, a solitary, dying aspen, you will be able to see beyond the broad Cement Creek Valley to the snowfields of Horse Basin and just the edge of Cement Mountain's north bowl.

Begin the drop by bearing west-southwest down the power line swath, then stay in the bottom of Walrod Gulch, shussing from one plateau to the next. **Cross quickly and singly over avalanche run-outs after 2.1 miles.** Freedom Of The Hills guide Don West remembers when the carcasses of two elk, apparently trapped and killed by an avalanche here, were found in the run-out in spring. Continue the easy descent past a right fork at mile 2.5, pass several private cabins, and come to the Cement Creek Road at mile 3.0.

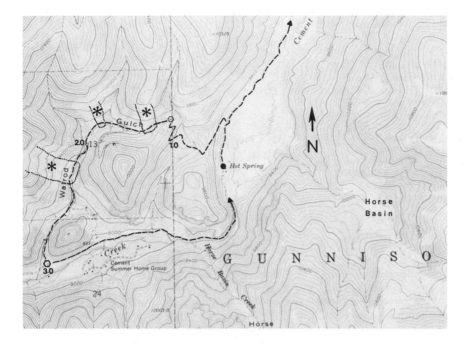

"Lunch tree"

27 COAL CREEK ROAD

One day trip
Terrain: Easiest
Distance: 4.7 miles /7.6 KM. one way
Skiing time: 3½-4 hours one way
Elevation gain: 625 feet /191 M.
Maximum elevation: 9,835 feet /2,998 M.
Season: Late November through mid-April
Topographic map:
   U.S.G.S. Mt. Axtell, Colo. 1961
Taylor River Ranger District
Gunnison National Forest

On any day in mid-winter a variety of ski tourers, each with a different objective or destination, might be seen on the Coal Creek Road. Crested Butte locals, decked out in running suits and racing skis, often ski the snow-packed road for a quick workout since it is only a couple miles from town. Others who want a more secluded, leisurely tour follow the road for a mile or so, then drop onto the Coal creekbed and loop back to the parking area. Overnighters, carrying a larger pack and using heavier skis, travel the road also as access to farther destinations: Splains Gulch (No. 28), Lily Lake and Floresta (No. 29), and Lake Irwin (No. 30). A snow machine from the Lake Irwin Lodge is currently being driven over the road about twice a week, ferrying customers and supplies to and from the lodge, and thus packs the roadbed into a faster, easier route for both ski tourers and snowmobilers.

Near the start of the tour the pointed top of Mt. Crested Butte shows prominently down the road (east), framed by the Coal Creek Valley. This famous landmark was named by Col. Ferdinand Hayden or members of his Geological Survey in 1874 for the band of sharp rock outcroppings below the summit which reminded the survey of a Spanish helmet.

Drive on Colo. 135 to Crested Butte, turn left (west) onto White Rock Avenue (two blocks south of Elk Avenue) and proceed five blocks to the 1st Street intersection. Continue west on the Coal Creek Road for another 1.7 miles to the Keystone Mine Road junction, the point of road closure by late November or so. Park carefully off the road.

Take the lower, left road where the Keystone Mine Road forks right and begin gliding west, soon crossing through a gate which marks the Gunnison National Forest boundary. Proceed high above Coal Creek, skirting an open hillside with scattered sage and aspen. Ski into stands of lodgepole pine after 1.1 miles and pass good views of 12,055-foot Mt. Axtell south, a long, snowy range fringed with conifers and flanked by a series of ridges and cirques. Bend right after 1.6 miles, curve left around an open hillside, then curve left again near 2.0 miles and pass a large avalanche run-out from Mt. Axtell, now partially grown in with trees. Continue west with long, easy glides as the creek rises to road level, pass the obvious opening of Splains Gulch (south) at 3.0 miles, and come to an open hillside in another 0.3 mile where the Splains Gulch road turns left across the creek (see No. 28).

Make an inconspicuous crossing of Coal Creek at 3.5 miles, enter an open, sometimes windy park, then re-cross the creek at mile 3.9 and pass an old log cabin farther left. Curve northwest as the drifted snowfields near Kebler Pass come into view and glide several hundred more yards to the Floresta/Lake Irwin road forks at 4.7 miles, marked by highway stakes with reflectorized extensions. Here the view extends about 3 miles southwest to the spectacular rock-and-snow Anthracite Range, highest near the spacious amphitheater and 12,271-foot summit of Ohio Peak at 200°/SSW. For extended tour routes from this junction, see Lily Lake and Floresta (No. 29) and Lake Irwin (No. 30).

Coal Creek Road/Crested Butte backdrop

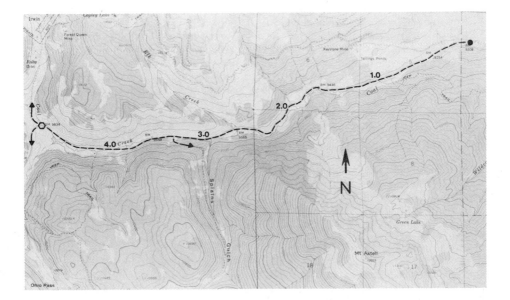

28 SPLAINS GULCH

One day trip or overnight
Terrain: Easiest
Distance: 4.4 miles/7.1 KM. one way
Skiing time: 3-3½ hours one way
Accum. elevation gain: 760 feet/232 M.
Accum. elevation loss: 470 feet/143 M.
Maximum elevation: 10,420 feet/3,176 M.
Season: Early November and late April
Topographic map:
**   U.S.G.S. Mt. Axtell, Colo. 1961**
Taylor River Ranger District
Gunnison National Forest

Deep powder skiing and beautiful views of The Castles in the West Elk Mountains highlight the tour south through Splains Gulch. The trip is usually done in early November after the first snowfalls but before Coal Creek Road has been closed for the winter, and then again in late April after the road has been plowed open. The most common route, described below, begins on the Splains Gulch Road, 3.3 miles from the Keystone Mine Road junction, and loops south past the deep Splains Gulch drainage to lookouts and north-facing powder fields. This route crosses two potential avalanche paths after mile 0.4 (see map photo) which are usually safe in early winter but pose an unacceptable risk with the deeper snow in mid-winter. **Never cross these paths after periods of snow and wind when avalanche danger is high.** For current avalanche conditions, contact the Crested Butte Ski Area, telephone (303) 349-6611. The other, "backdoor" entrance, also an ending point on a tour loop, begins east of the sawdust pile, about 5.6 miles from the Keystone Mine Road. After a short, steep uphill, this route, almost always safe from avalanche, climbs easily along a drainage-way, linking several beautiful, snow-blanketed parks not shown on the topo.

Drive on Colo. 135 to Crested Butte, turn left (west) onto White Rock Avenue (two blocks south of Elk Avenue) and proceed five blocks to the 1st Street intersection. Continue west on the Coal Creek Road for another 1.7 miles to the Keystone Mine Road junction, the usual point of road closure by late November. For early winter and late spring tours, follow the Coal Creek Road for another 3.3 miles to the Splains Gulch drop-off, turn left after 4.7 miles where another road forks right toward Irwin, and come to the usual parking and pick-up spot at the sawdust pile, a total of 5.6 miles from the Keystone Mine Road junction.

For the midwinter tour route, follow paragraph four of the Coal Creek Road tour (No. 27). Pick up Splains Gulch Road at the far end of the open hillside, swing east on a gradual traverse through thick conifers, and pass an old mine building right and tracks left after 0.3 mile. Bend south in 40 more yards into the sun, **cross quickly and singly over two avalanche paths after 0.4 and 0.7 mile, observing precautions even if danger is low,** and continue south up the quiet, scenic corridor through spruce and fir. Pass a tributary which joins Splains Creek in a snowy park (left) at mile 1.2, break trail on a more level course, curving right past the 12,638-foot mountain, and enter a more open basin after 2.0 miles. In view through this section is the snowy bowl on Mt. Axtell behind at 63°/ENE, then four, snow-capped summits in the Anthracite Range, highest near 12,271-foot Ohio Peak at 235°/WSW, and a white, sparsely-covered mound at 252°/W to the right of a conspicuous cirque.

Contour southwest for 0.3 mile to a slight saddle, then loop east toward the top of the 12,638-foot mountain for an engaging vista of The Castles in the West Elk Mountains at 200°/SSW and for a return run north through scattered trees and powder fields (see map). To continue to the pick-up point near Kebler Pass, stay in the open basin at 2.0 miles, break trail west across Lost Lake, then pass another park at 2.8 miles which extends south and follow treeline (right) back onto the road-cut. Begin a slight drop northwest through deep, snow-laden evergreens, passing occasional glimpses of the Anthracite Range left. Break into a small park, unmarked on the topo, bear north-northeast into more open clearings filled with large snow mounds, and pick up an obvious, open drainage (left) after 3.7 miles. Begin dropping again as the drainage fills with trees, swing right on a steep downhill traverse at mile 4.3, and break into the open basin near the sawdust pile, the pick-up point for early winter and spring tours. For midwinter touring, continue north — often over snowmobile tracks — to the Coal Creek Road junction.

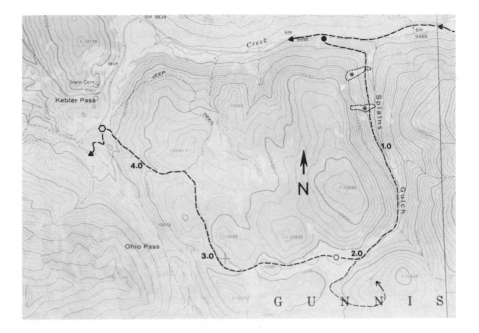

Avalanche test

29 LILY LAKE AND FLORESTA

Half-day trip or overnight
Terrain: Easiest to most difficult
Distance: 2.0 miles/3.2 KM. one way
Skiing time: 1-1½ hours one way
Accum. elevation gain: 300 feet/91 M.
Accum. elevation loss: 330 feet/101 M.
Maximum elevation: 10,190 feet/3,106 M.
Season: Early November and late April
Topographic maps:
  U.S.G.S. Mt. Axtell, Colo. 1961
  U.S.G.S. Anthracite Range, Colo. 1961
Taylor River Ranger District
Gunnison National Forest

The tour route to the snow-covered basin of Lily Lake penetrates thick stands of spruce for the first mile, then breaks out beneath a sparsely-covered, north-facing hillside, the perfect area to practice downhill christies and telemarks. The tour can be continued beyond Lily Lake with a steep, southerly drop to the old mining camp of Floresta (now gone), as figured for the information capsule, and then looped north and east around the ''10,310''-foot hill via the old railroad grade. However, in early winter when this longer loop receives the most traffic, the downhill section to Floresta often becomes icy and very fast, sometimes most easily managed by carrying skis and hiking for several hundred yards.

In winter Lily Lake and Floresta become remote, overnight destinations, reached after a long tour up the Coal Creek Road (No. 27). Trail-breaking begins usually from the sawdust pile after 5.6 miles which is also the starting point for the tour in early winter and late spring when the Coal Creek Road has been plowed open. Deep snow — often too deep for the snowmobiles from Irwin Lodge — makes access a one-step-at-a-time job but it also makes dazzling-white monuments of the surrounding high ranges and decorates the nearby hillsides and valleys with free-form sculptures, providing winter impressions to last a lifetime. Old-timers who lived in the area while the Floresta Coal Mine was

operating remember the incredible snow depth in winter. One, as recorded in Wolle's *Stampede to Timberline*, recalled his days of driving horse-drawn freight wagons to Floresta over the snow-**packed** road. ''In the summer it looked funny to see those rubbed scars (on the trees which lined the road) twenty-five feet up in the air, but in the winter the road was that high up.''

Follow driving instructions for the Coal Creek Road tour (No. 27), proceeding west from Crested Butte to road closure at the Keystone Mine Road junction. For early winter and late spring tours when the road has been plowed, continue west on the Coal Creek Road for 4.7 miles to the Lake Irwin/Kebler Pass Road junction. Fork left, stay left where the Kebler Pass Road angles right, and come to the usual parking spot at the sawdust pile, a total of 5.6 miles from the Keystone Mine Road junction.

From the sawdust pile — a 20-foot high, snow-covered mound — bear south, then west on a loop across a branch of Ruby Anthracite Creek. Follow the roadcut on a hillside contour above the creek drainage (right), enter the trees near 0.5 mile and stay right in another 35 yards where an apparent opening leads left on a climb. Loop through a conspicuous drainage, then follow the north-facing roadcut through a section of dense, shady spruce, and break onto a sparsely-covered hillside after 1.0 mile, a good down-hilling area (see map). Climb to a crossing of Lily Lake Creek and break trail west past a metal shack and barbed wire fence (which shows in early winter) to the flat Lily lakebed at 1.3 miles. From each opening in the trees on this first mile the view extends north to the scalloped ridges and cirques of Scarp Ridge, a truly spectacular panorama.

To continue to the Floresta site, cross to the west side of Lily Lake and pick up the roadcut in the trees. Soon break out to a splendid view of the Ruby Anthracite Creek Valley and the snow-topped summits of the Anthracite Range southwest; turn left toward the range and use a strong snowplow and pole drag to manage the two steep drops to the open basin below Floresta. Connect with the northerly cut of the old railroad grade, more visible in the trees, proceed over the gently rolling course toward the Ruby Range and Scarp Ridge, and eventually loop southeast to the stopping point at the sawdust pile, a round trip distance of 5.2 miles.

Igloo construction

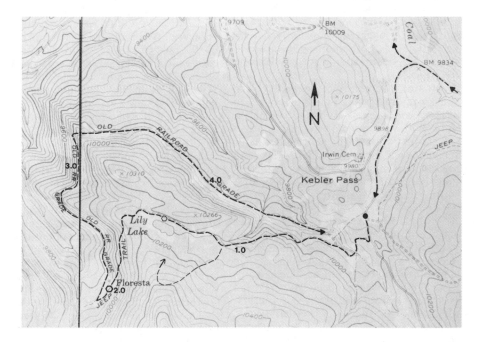

30 LAKE IRWIN

Half-day trip or overnight
Terrain: More difficult
Distance: 1.7 miles/2.7 KM. one way
Skiing time: 1½-2 hours one way
Elevation gain: 490 feet/149 M.
Maximum elevation: 10,420 feet/3,176 M.
Season: Early November and late April
Topographic maps:
   U.S.G.S. Mt. Axtell, Colo. 1961
   U.S.G.S. Oh-Be-Joyful, Colo. 1961
Taylor River Ranger District
Gunnison National Forest

Like Splains Gulch (No. 28) and Lily Lake and Floresta (No. 29), the Lake Irwin tour is usually done as a half-day trip in early November before Coal Creek Road has been closed and again in mid-April or so after it has been plowed open. In winter the tour becomes an extended, overnight trip with access via the snow-machine-packed Coal Creek roadbed (No. 27). The newly-built, massive Irwin Lodge north of Lake Irwin, for which the road is packed as supplies and guests are ferried in from Crested Butte, makes an unusual landmark among the surrounding pristine wilderness of Scarp Ridge and the Ruby Range and serves as a possible destination for the tour. The lodge currently provides accomodations for both snowmobile and ski tour groups, reservations only, telephone (303) 349-5140.

Snow and skiers are nothing new to the Lake Irwin area, according to accounts in Wolle's *Stampede to Timberline*. When the nearby Ruby mining camp boomed to life in 1879, the first winter residents watched snow after snow fall from the leaden skies until snow cover eventually reached 50 feet, completely burying all cabins and mine buildings. The following spring an eager party of prospectors mushed into the camp, probably skiing on "Norwegian snowshoes," and although sure they were near the camp, they could find no cabins. Finally spotting a man standing by a smoking hole in the snow, they asked him where the camp was located.

"You're in it," he replied. "Where's the post office?" asked one of the prospectors. "Right in the next hole, sir," was the answer.

Old-timers who lived in the area recall winters when the snow cover allowed them to ski off the roofs of their cabins. Bill Kerr of the Taylor River Ranger District, who grew up during the early days in Crested Butte, remembers clearly his ski trips in the '30's along the Coal Creek Road to Irwin, as well as to Gothic (No. 32) and to Baxter Gulch south of Crested Butte. There were no fancy wood laminate or fiberglass skis in those days. However, Bill got along well with homemade pine skis, steamed to a curved tip, a leather strap for a binding, and one stout pole. "The skis were waxed to high heavens with parafin off the jelly jars," he recalls.

Follow driving instructions for the Coal Creek Road tour (No. 27), proceeding west from Crested Butte to road closure at the Keystone Mine Road junction. For early winter and late spring tours when the road has been plowed, continue west on the Coal Creek Road for 4.7 miles to the junction with the unplowed road to Lake Irwin. Park carefully along the Coal Creek Road.

Swing north onto the unplowed Coal Creek Road, marked by highway stakes with reflectorized extensions, and proceed on a gradual climb into a wide basin, staying left of the creekbed. (Snow-machine tracks may fork left toward the Ruby Anthracite Creek Valley, an alternate route which is also used by snowmobiles.) Pass the Ruby site after 0.7 mile where old stone walls show sometimes in early winter, climb more noticeably past a cabin (right) near the Irwin site, and continue north across Coal Creek passing the private cabins and mining structures of the Forest Queen, Irwin's most famous silver mine. With the gain in elevation, a beautiful panorama of snow-clad peaks and ridges can be seen on the horizon. A series of sharp ridges and cirques, with a high point at 12,271-foot Ohio Peak, form the Anthracite Range behind. And ahead the virgin, Alp-like summits of Scarp Ridge lead west toward the Ruby Range, a vista that is the highlight of the tour.

Curve northwest with the hillside contour after 1.1 miles, follow the roadcut through a patch of conifers and break out onto the huge Irwin lakebed at mile 1.7, a good destination for a half-day tour. (The route to Irwin Lodge circles the south side of the lake.) For the return, a short loop can be made by skiing south from the lake over the "10,445" hill, then downhilling to the main trail (see map), a highly recommended route when light powder snow covers the hillside.

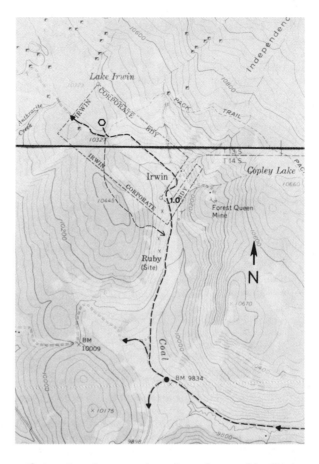

Olden day skiers — photo from George MacKeen

31 WASHINGTON GULCH

One day trip or overnight
Terrain: Easiest through most difficult
Distance: 5.2 miles/8.4 KM. one way
Skiing time: 3½-4½ hours one way
Accum. elevation gain: 1,170 feet/357 M.
Accum. elevation loss: 60 feet/18 M.
Maximum elevation: 10,450 feet/3,185 M.
Season: Mid-November through April
Topographic maps:
   U.S.G.S. Gothic, Colo. 1961
   U.S.G.S. Oh-Be-Joyful, Colo. 1961
Taylor River Ranger District
Gunnison National Forest

The tour up Washington Gulch, featured often in newspaper and ski magazine articles, rates as the most popular route in the Crested Butte area, due in part to its proximity to the Crested Butte Ski Area. The main tour route on the Washington Gulch Road, described below, receives daily skier traffic when the weather is good, and usually has a hard, well-broken track, an ideal aid to technique training for both beginners and racers. Other routes are charted along the west side of Washington Creek and up and down the aspen-covered hillside east of Meridian Lake. Day tourers usually follow the roadbed through easy-gliding, rolling terrain for two or three miles, and overnighters continue farther through moderate but steady climbs to the private cabins of Elkton, the destination figured in the information capsule. For cabin reservations, contact: The Alpineer, P.O. Box 208, Crested Butte, CO 81224, telephone: (303) 349-5210. Pick a clear-weather day for the tour because little protection from wind exists in the wide, treeless gulch.

Besides good skiing, the Washington Gulch tour offers good views of the area's unusual mountains. Crested Butte, girded with the sharp, rock spires for which it is named, provides a scenic backdrop near the trailhead at 114°/SE. Snow-capped tops, one possibly Mineral Point at 295°/NW and another the long, southeasterly ridge from Purple Mountain at 301°/NW, give hints of the spectacular Ruby Range beyond. And the blunt top and large ravine of Gothic Mountain, named undoubtedly for its bold, imposing appearance, shows down the gulch at 332°/NNW.

Drive on Colo. 135 to Crested Butte, then proceed north from the junction with the main street (Elk Avenue) for another 1.8 miles to the Washington Gulch Road, marked by a sign reading "Meridian Lake development." Turn left (northwest) onto the gravel road and continue to snow closure, usually another 2.1 miles by mid-November. Park carefully in the turn-around area.

Begin skiing northwest from snow closure on a long, downhill coast, passing through a fence. Follow the roadbed up the flat, treeless gulch with long, easy glides: continue northwest toward the snowy top of Purple Mountain for the first mile, then swing slightly right and bear toward rugged Gothic Mountain. Stay on the roadbed past a private A-frame (left) after 2.3 miles, pass through a barbed wire fence in another 40 yards near the first clump of trees on the route, and come to the top of a hill, a good destination point for a short, one-day tour. Here the barest, rocky tops of White Rock Mountain show through the Snodgrass and Gothic Mountain saddle at 47°/ENE.

Loop right, then left on the roadbed or make a short drop and climb on a shortcut after 2.5 miles. Proceed on gradual, steady climbs high above the valley floor (left), pass thick banks of conifers then open, snowy ravines on the far valley wall beneath Anthracite Mesa, and cross a spruce-filled ravine near 3.5 miles that comes down from Gothic Mountain. Continue north after 4.0 miles along the westerly reaches of Gothic Mountain, swing left, then right around the Elkton ridge at mile 4.8, and make the final, steep climb north to the Elkton cabins. From the 10,200-foot-plus lookouts on this last section, a panorama of dark green ridges and white peaks appears through the valley. Most imposing is Gothic Mountain with the north summit, banded by rock outcroppings, in view now at 80°/E. Crested Butte shows beyond the vast, white valley floor at 124°/SE, and Mount Emmons at the east end of Scarp Ridge, beautifully striated with layers of rock, makes an appearance at 171°/S.

Before the fall

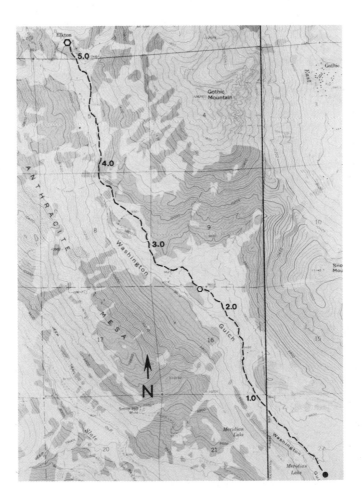

32 GOTHIC

One day trip
Terrain: Easiest
Distance: 5.0 miles/8.0 KM.
Skiing time: 3-3½ hours one way
Accum. elevation gain: 290 feet/88 M.
Accum. elevation loss: 280 feet/85 M.
Maximum elevation: 9,640 feet/2,938 M.
Season: Mid-November through April
Topographic map:
  U.S.G.S. Gothic, Colo. 1961
Taylor River Ranger District
Gunnison National Forest

Like the Washington Gulch tour (No. 31), the trip to the old mining camp of Gothic penetrates a wide, mostly-open, northeasterly valley, ending up on the other side of Gothic Mountain from Elkton. This route offers even easier ski terrain than does Washington Gulch, due to the very slight gains and losses in elevation, but also includes one major obstacle: avalanche. The major paths, drafted on the map photo, can be seen on the northeast side of Snodgrass and Gothic Mountains; other small but equally-dangerous sluffs line the roadway. **Thus, this route should be taken only when potential danger is very low by skiers who recognize avalanche conditions.** See Avalanche Recognition and Rules in the Introduction. For current avalanche conditions, phone the Taylor River Ranger District in Gunnison at (303) 641-0471 or the Crested Butte Ski Area at 349-6611. Extended trips beyond Gothic to Schofield Pass via the East River Valley and to East Maroon Pass via the Copper Creek Valley, sometimes attempted in spring, require electronic signalling devices, snow shovel, avalanche cord, etc., trips best done with the aid of an RMSIA Certified Mountain Ski Touring Guide.

The mining camp of Gothic, now nearly deserted, sprang to life in the summer of 1879 during Colorado's silver rush days. In *Crofutt's 1885 Grip-Sack Guide of Colorado*, the author catalogued the "town" with these words: "It is an outfitting point for many small mining camps in the vicinity, and hundreds of prospectors who are picking into the mountains in every direction. The town is liberally supplied with stores, hotels, and shops of all kinds, one weekly newspaper, the *Silver Record*, one smelting works, three saw-mills, churches, schools, etc."

From the earliest days, avalanches and snow were a memorable part of life in Gothic, according to Muriel Sibell Wolle in *Stampede to Timberline*. One old-timer remembered: "So many miners were lost in slides that women used to tell their fathers, husbands and brothers goodbye when they left for the mines each day, fearing that they might never see them again. . .

Everybody in town wore snowshoes a good part of the year." Today most of the original log cabins in Gothic have collapsed or have been torn down. The few remaining — weathered, wind-scarred, and quiet — bear testimony to the many miners who struggled to live in this high and wild place.

Drive on Colo. 135 to Crested Butte; continue north from the junction with the main street (Elk Avenue), pass the Washington Gulch turnoff after 1.8 miles and the Crested Butte Ski Area after 2.7 miles. Proceed on the main road to snow closure, usually another 0.8 mile beyond the ski area, and park carefully near the turn-around. In early winter the road may be plowed another 0.9 mile to the Crested Butte Stables.

Begin gliding up the unplowed East River Road; ski away from the Crested Butte Ski Area runs, pass several houses (right), and continue toward a restful, blue-and-white panorama of Avery Peak north and the White Rock Range across the valley northeast. Ski by a small building (right) at 0.9 mile with a sign reading "Crested Butte Stables," a possible point for road closure in future years. Soon cross the National Forest boundary and come to a possible turn-off east to the roadbed which follows the right side of the East River Valley, an alternate route if avalanche danger is high (see map). **Continue on the East River Road only if avalanche conditions are low:** make an easy, up-and-down traverse for three miles along the aspen-covered side of Snodgrass and Gothic Mountain. Drop and climb across the East River at 4.4 miles, follow the roadbed north and proceed down the main street of Gothic at mile 4.8, passing a few old, some new private buildings. An obvious roadbed which climbs right (east) into the Copper Creek Valley, marked "Vehicular Travel Not Advised," etc. makes a good destination for a long, one-day tour. Return over the ski tracks on the fast, rolling course.

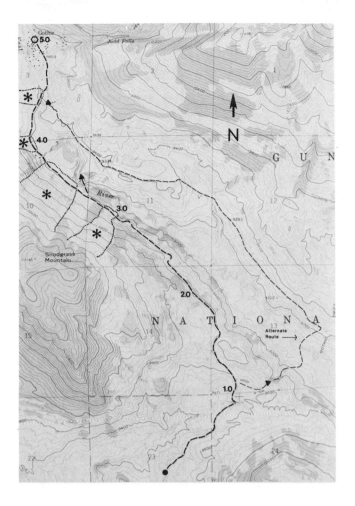

Gothic grandeur

33 BRUSH CREEK AND PEARL PASS

Half-day trip to overnight
Terrain: Easiest to most difficult
Distance: 12.5 miles/20.1 KM. one way
Skiing time: 7-9 hours one way
Accum. elevation gain: 4,125 feet/1,257 M.
Accum. elevation loss: 340 feet/104 M.
Maximum elevation: 12,705 feet/3,872 M.
Season: Mid-November through April
Topographic maps:
   U.S.G.S Crested Butte, Colo. 1961
   U.S.G.S. Gothic, Colo. 1961
   U.S.G.S. Pearl Pass, Colo. 1961
Taylor River Ranger District
Gunnison National Forest

A tour over the snow-covered Brush Creek Road can be anything from a half-day trip of a mile or two to part of a two- or three-day winter expedition, a very advanced but increasingly popular trek of about 20 miles and 4,125 feet of elevation gain to Ashcroft via Pearl Pass. Similar to the well-known tour from the Lake Eldora Ski Area to Winter Park via Rollins Pass (**Colorado Front Range Ski Tours** No. 11), this "Crested Butte to Aspen" route appeals to one's sense of expediency because it links directly two mountain towns otherwise connected by over 270 miles of driving. Some tourers travel from Aspen to Crested Butte which allows for a base camp at the Tagert Hut and makes a long downhill run from Pearl Pass to snow closure on the Brush Creek Road, the longest part of the trip (see Tagert Hut and Pearl Pass No. 34). Others make the trip one way, visit their neighbors on the other side of the mountain, then ski back home. RMSIA Certified Guides are available in Crested Butte and Aspen.

Here is the usual **modus operandi** for the tour: **1.** Be extremely cautious of bad weather hazards such as whiteouts, cold temperatures, and avalanche (note avalanche paths on map). **Never attempt the tour when avalanche conditions are high or when bad wea-** **ther is threatening.** For current avalanche conditions, call the Crested Butte Ski Area at (303) 349-6611. **2.** Leave name and estimated arrival time for emergency-only search and rescue in Crested Butte at The Alpineer, telephone 349-5210, in Aspen with Mr. Fred Braun, telephone 925-7162. **3.** Draft course, as shown on map photo, onto the Pearl Pass and Hayden Peak topos (see also No. 34); use compass and follow course carefully. **4.** Start early on the first day; follow the Brush Creek and East Brush Creek Valleys, as described, on an 11-mile climb to timberline, the usual first night's camp. **5. Proceed only if weather permits;** follow a cross-country course north on a slight ridge between the right and left tributaries of East Brush Creek for 0.5 mile, then swing northwest toward the Pearl Pass saddle; **do not follow the right or left tributaries. 6.** From Pearl Pass, use compass to swing northwest above Pearl Basin/Cooper Creek drainage; **do not drop into the Cooper Creek drainage.** Either ski to Ashcroft on the second day, or pitch a tent or dig a snow cave in upper Pearl Basin, and make the exciting descent on the third day. **7.** Arrange for a car pick-up at Ashcroft, or take the shuttle buses to the Aspen airport and fly back over the range via

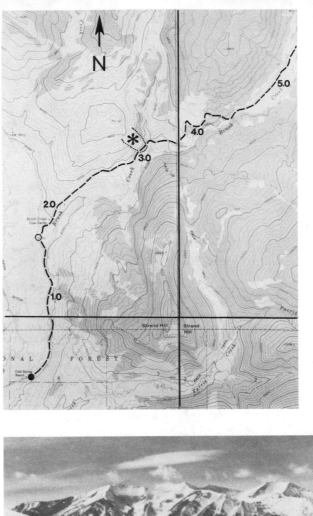

Beyond Whetstone Mountain

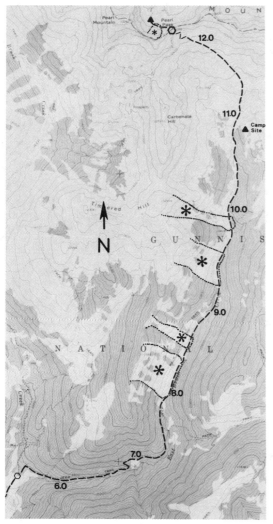

Crested Butte Air Service. Flies daily, weather permitting, telephone 349-5303.

Drive northwest on Colo. 135 toward Crested Butte to the Brush Creek Road marked by a sign. From Crested Butte (jct. with Elk Avenue) drive southeast for 2.1 miles beyond the Slate River bridge. Turn northeast, proceed past the airport turnoff after 1.1 miles, and continue to road closure usually near the Cold Spring Ranch, a total of 3.1 miles from Colo. 135. Park carefully near the turnaround.

Follow the wide, snowy roadbed northeast, then north from Cold Spring Ranch for 1.6 miles to the Brush Creek Road junction, a delightful, well-used tour for beginners. Fork right onto the Brush Creek Road, marked by a sign; pass through the Brush Creek Cow Camp, stay right after 2.6 miles where the West Brush Creek Trail forks left, and proceed with caution under a slide area. Take the far left, unsigned fork on a steep climb at 3.5 miles, pass the Teocalli Ridge Trail at mile 4.0, then proceed northeast through Brush Creek Park and fork right at 5.5 miles onto the East Brush Creek Trail, a good lunch destination. Continue east and north on a cross-country course along the right side of East Brush Creek, avoiding the avalanche paths from Timbered and Carbonate Hills. For the first night's camp, find open water below timberline near mile 11.0. Follow the cross-country course north, then northwest to Pearl Pass, as marked on the map. The view: top-of-the-world!

34 TAGERT HUT AND PEARL PASS

One day trips or overnights
Terrain: Most difficult
Season: Mid-November through April
Topographic maps:
 U.S.G.S. Hayden Peak, Colo. 1960
 U.S.G.S. Pearl Pass, Colo. 1961
Aspen Ranger District
White River National Forest

In 1882, when Ashcroft boomed as a silver mining camp, a celebrated stage and freight road was pushed over the 12,705-foot top of Pearl Pass, providing a much more direct link with Crested Butte and its railroad than the Taylor Pass Toll Road. Teams of burros pulled ore wagons and supplies over the range, and soon a regular stage line began operating, ferrying prospectors, speculators, dandies, and dancing girls to and from the bustling camp. When the Denver and Rio Grande Railroad reached Aspen in 1887 however, Ashcroft, already dying, lost even more population, and the famed Pearl Pass Road eventually dwindled to a "jack trail." According to Wolle's *Stampede To Timberline*, the range was crossed in winter by a mail carrier in those early days. He was a tough veteran at the job but "he foundered over the hardest trail of all, Pearl Pass."

Today this same Pearl Pass trail is regaining its notoriety, this time as an advanced but often travelled "Aspen to Crested Butte" ski route. The tour begins from snow closure at the Ashcroft Ski Touring Area and climbs steeply up the Castle Creek Valley to the Tagert Hut at 5.0 miles, itself a popular destination and also a convenient base for the attempt over Pearl Pass. After a cross-country climb for about 2.6 miles through wintry artic-alpine snowfields to the pass, the tour route begins a 12.5 mile drop through the East Brush Creek and Brush Creek Valleys to snow closure on the Brush Creek Road. (See Brush Creek and Pearl Pass tour No. 33 for this downhill route and for an important list of procedures and dangers.) **Note the avalanche paths on the map and consider this tour only when danger is low.** For current avalanche conditions, phone the Aspen Ranger District at (303) 925-3445.

The Tagert Hut is a cozy, tin-roofed A-frame with an occupancy limit of eight persons, built by the Rocky Mountain School of Carbondale, Fred Braun, and other voluntary help. It stands as a memorial to pioneer William "Billy" Tagert who drove a stage and freight wagon over Taylor Pass to Dorchester during silver rush days, ran a stable and livery service, then operated a ranch at Tagert Lake. He donated the one-third acre for the hut to the United States Ski Association. For information on reservations and regulations, see the Markley and Barnard Huts tour (No. 36).

From Colo. 82 turn south onto the Castle Creek Road and drive 11.7 miles to the Ashcroft Ski Touring Area parking lot, following instructions in the Lindley Hut tour (No. 35).

34A TAGERT HUT

Distance: 5.0 miles/8.0 KM. one way
Skiing time: 3½-4 hours one way
Elevation gain: 1,780 feet/543 M.
Maximum elevation: 11,280 feet/3,438 M.

First, ski to the Iron Mountain Road junction at mile 1.8, following paragraph five of the Lindley Hut tour (No. 35). Swing right onto the Castle Creek Road, marked also as the "Montezuma Road." Follow the rolling, public access roadbed through the south end of Ashcroft Ski Touring Area, then begin to climb steeply, passing these landmarks: a creek crossing at 3.1 miles, a steep climb southwest to another creek crossing and excellent vista point at 4.6 miles, a bend left then right to the Castle Creek/Montezuma Mine Road junction at 4.8 miles. Fork left at this junction onto the smaller pathway (usually broken by tracks) and come to the Tagert Hut in about 300 yards.

34B PEARL PASS

Distance: 7.6 miles/12.2 KM. one way
Skiing time: 7-8 hours one way
Elevation gain: 3,205 feet/997 M.
Maximum elevation: 12,705 feet/3,872 M.

To continue the final 2.6 miles to Pearl Pass, head south into Castle Creek Bowl, then veer southeast; stay above the summer trail and below avalanche danger, and avoid the false passes to Middle Brush Creek.

Tagert hut

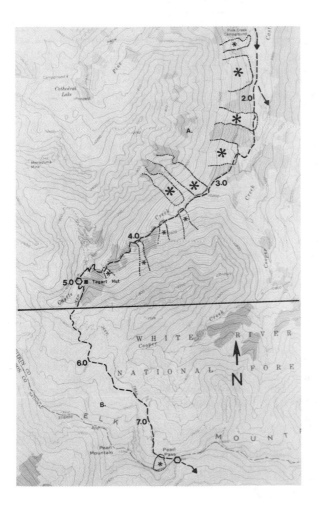

35 LINDLEY HUT

One day trip or overnight
Terrain: More difficult
Distance: 3.8 miles/6.1 KM. one way
Skiing time: 2-2½ hours one way
Accum. elevation gain: 1,020 feet/311 M.
Accum. elevation loss: 80 feet/24 M.
Maximum elevation: 10,520 feet/3,206 M.
Season: Mid-November through April
Topographic map:
** U.S.G.S. Hayden Peak, Colo. 1960**
Aspen Ranger District
White River National Forest

Of the five tours to Braun Huts in the Ashcroft area, the Lindley Hut tour via Iron Mountain Road offers the easiest route, making it a popular choice for tour groups of mixed abilities. The tour begins with a level, warm-up run of 1.8 miles up the Castle Creek Valley to a junction where the Iron Mountain Road forks left and the Castle Creek Road — the Tagert Hut tour route (No. 34) — continues right. This first section, often packed and set with a track, is a favorite touring area for both beginners and cross-country racers. Others are headed for Ashcroft's Pine Creek Cookhouse restaurant at mile 1.2. Except for a short drop to the hut itself, the remaining 2.0 miles of roadbed maintain a steady climb of 8% grade, enough to provide a zipping return but with adequate room for snowplow control. **An avalanche path, usually posted by sign, intercepts the route near mile 3.0 and should be crossed only during periods of stability.** For avalanche information, phone the Aspen Ranger District at (303) 925-3445.

The Lindley Hut, largest of the Braun Huts, is an imposing structure of gray cinder blocks, spacious enough for up to twenty persons. It was designed and built by Fred Braun in 1973 in memory of Mr. Alfred Lindley, replacing an earlier cabin which burned, and is comfortably furnished with a pot-bellied stove, fireplace, limited firewood, tables and beds, etc. For information on reservations and regulations, see the Markley and Barnard Huts tour (No. 36).

Note: Access to the Braun Huts crosses through the commercial Ashcroft Ski Touring Area to the White River National Forest via well-posted public right-of-ways. Do not ski on the Ashcroft ski trails without a trail ticket. Overnighters who park in the Ashcroft parking lot should leave keys at the Ashcroft Headquarters in the King Cabin so the parking lot can be plowed.

Drive on Colo. 82 to the Maroon Lake/Ashcroft Road west of Aspen, marked by a sign (0.4 mile west of the Castle Creek bridge). Turn south, immediately turn left where the Maroon Lake Road forks right, and continue for 11.7 miles to the Ashcroft Ski Touring Area parking lot on the left side of the road. Park here and walk the remaining 150 yards of plowed road to the trailhead near the Ashcroft Headquarters.

Begin skiing south over the flat Castle Creek roadbed, passing above the restored cabins and false front buildings of the Ashcroft ghost town. Break through a scattering of aspen after 0.4 mile where a magnificent vista of Elk Mountains unfolds at the end of the valley. Soon pass the Cathedral Lake Trail turnoff (usually closed in winter), which brings Cathedral Peak into view at 236°/WSW, and continue over a rise to the Pine Creek Cookhouse turnoff at mile 1.2. From left to right, the panorama of the Elk Mountains, often backlit and shimmering in the midday sun, now includes the white Star Bowl, the 13,521-foot Star Peak at 160°/S, the broad snowfields of Cooper Bowl, then Iron Mountain at 185°/SSW, and the obvious Castle Creek Valley to the right. Glide past the orange-yellow willows in Castle Creek left, and after 1.8 miles come to the junction with the Iron Mountain Road, ending the "easiest" tour.

Fork left across the open basin, cross Castle Creek above the bridge, then pass below private buildings and equipment of the iron mine and make a short climb back to the road. Climb gradually up the wide roadbed, gaining better and better views of the pillared and striated Elk Mountains west and south. **Observe avalanche procedures on crossing the slide path at mile 3.0,** fork right off the road at the first switchback at 3.6 miles, and make a 0.2 mile descent to the Lindley Hut. Extensions for the tour: a new route, **proposal stage only,** up Cooper Creek to Pearl Pass, or a continuation of 2 miles on the Iron Mountain Road with a 1,000-foot, cross-country return drop.

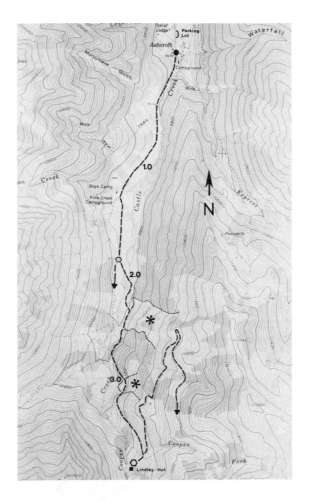

Castle Creek Valley view

36 MARKLEY AND BARNARD HUTS

One day trips or overnights
Terrain: Most difficult
Season: Mid-November through April
Topographic maps:
 U.S.G.S. Hayden Peak, Colo. 1960
 U.S.G.S. New York Peak, Colo. 1960
Aspen Ranger District
White River National Forest

The Alfred E. Braun Hut System, a collection of unique winter cabins in the Elk Mountains above Aspen and Ashcroft, gives opportunity to explore one of the most stunningly beautiful regions of Colorado. Of the tours in the guidebook, only the Trail of the Tenth (No. 12) has vistas which rival those seen along the Barnard Hut trail or from Pearl Pass (No's. 33 and 34). Under United States Ski Association auspices, these cabins were designed and built mostly, and are maintained by Aspenite, ski mountaineer Fred Braun, who has spent hundreds of voluntary hours on the system. For example, the Barnard Hut, a memorial to Mr. Marshall Barnard, has bedrooms, sundeck, and stone-masoned footings and was designed and built by Braun, Paul Wirth, and other voluntary help with the use of hand tools only.

All huts contain a stove and fireplace, limited firewood, bunks and mattresses, kitchen utensils, and privy, and can be reserved for about $3 per person per day. For reservations, usually needed about one month in advance, contact Mr. Fred Braun, USSA Hut Committee Chairman, 702 W. Main St., Aspen, CO 81611, telephone (303) 925-7162. Send a 20% deposit with reservation; pay the balance (no credit cards) and pick up the keys from Mr. Braun before the trip. For further information, contact the Aspen Ranger District, 806 W. Hallam in Aspen, telephone 925-3445.

Please treat the huts with care and remember these few, common-sense procedures: 1. Be frugal with firewood, chop outside, store axe inside. 2. Store food in mouse-proof containers. 3. Leave floors, tables, and beds clean and neat. 4. Scald kitchen utensils. 5. Empty water from pots so they don't freeze and break. 6. Use small amount of lime in privy. 7. Lock all doors and windows against snow and vandals. Useful donations include paper towels and cloths for cleaning, extra firewood, candles.

Drive on Colo. 82 to the Maroon Lake/Ashcroft Road west of Aspen, marked by a sign (0.4 mile west of the Castle Creek bridge). Turn south, immediately turn left where the Maroon Lake Road forks right, and continue for 11.7 miles to the Ashcroft Ski Touring Area parking lot on the left side of the road. Or ride the convenient Pitkin County and Ashcroft buses to the area. Overnighters should check car keys and obtain weather and avalanche information at Ashcroft Headquarters in the King Cabin, 150 yards up the road at snow closure.

36A MARKLEY HUT

Distance: 2.2 miles/3.5 KM. one way
Skiing time: 1½-2 hours one way
Elevation gain: 1,000 feet/305 M.
Maximum elevation: 10,400 feet/3,170 M.

Although a steep climb in and a fast run out, often over a snowmobile-packed course, the tour to the Markley Hut measures only 2.2 miles, often a destination for persistent novices who prevail over the crash-and-burn stops on the return. The picturesque A-frame, built in memory of Mrs. Edna Markley, holds eight persons maximum and serves also as a base for advanced skiers who continue to the Barnard or Goodwin-Greene Huts. Follow the Express Creek Road to a signed turnoff at mile 2.1, then drop to the hut near the creekbed (see map).

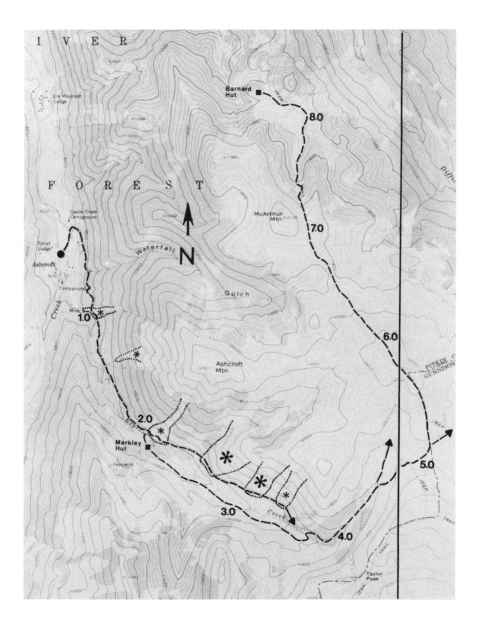

36B BARNARD HUT

Distance: 8.4 miles / 13.5 KM. one way
Skiing time: 7-8 hours one way
Accum. elevation gain: 3,030 feet / 924 M.
Accum. elevation loss: 1,000 feet / 305 M.
Maximum elevation: 12,300 feet / 3,749 M.

Voila! Barnard Hut

The Barnard Hut trip rates as one of the most difficult in this guidebook for its 8.4 mile distance, over-3,000-foot accumulated climb, and orienteering challenge through arctic-alpine snowfields. But for those in good shape, the physical exhilaration, the tremendous skiing, and best of all, the top-of-the-world view make this the tour of a lifetime. **Note avalanche hazards on map.** See the Goodwin-Greene Hut tour (No. 37) for details on the route.

37 GOODWIN-GREENE HUT

Overnight
Terrain: Most difficult
Distance: 7.5 miles/12.1 KM. one way
Skiing time: 6½-7½ hours one way
Accum. elevation gain: 2,720 feet/829 M.
Accum. elevation loss: 490 feet/149 M.
Maximum elevation: 12,120 feet/3,694 M.
Season: Mid-November through April
Topographic maps:
  U.S.G.S. Hayden Peak, Colo. 1960
  U.S.G.S. New York Peak, Colo. 1960
Aspen Ranger District
White River National Forest

Newest of the Braun Huts above Ashcroft and most elegant, the Swedish-log Goodwin-Greene Hut sits near timberline at the headwaters of Difficult Creek, below the open snowbanks of Gold Hill. It was built "in memory of two young men who loved these mountains," Peter Colt Goodwin and Carl Rollins Greene, who were killed in a climbing accident in November 1970 in the California Sierras. Like the trip to the Barnard Hut, this tour pushes high into the Elk Mountains and requires well-practiced orienteering and avalanche recognition skills, advanced ski technique and superb physical fitness, plus a day of clear weather. **Never attempt this tour after periods of snow and wind when avalanche danger is high.** For current avalanche conditions, call the Aspen Ranger District at (303) 925-3445. RMSIA Certified Mountain Ski Touring Guides are available in Aspen.

Together with the Markley and Barnard Huts (No. 36), the Goodwin-Greene Hut provides convenient, even luxurious overnight shelter to make possible an adventurous hut-to-hut tour, an extended trip of at least three and one-half days but safest and most enjoyable in four or five. The trip to the Goodwin-Greene Hut measures about 0.9 mile, 310 feet elevation gain **less** than the Barnard Hut trip, and thus serves as the slightly less difficult second-day destination from the Markley Hut. However, both trips are very challenging: only the magnificent view from the top of the Elk Mountain Range — west to the soaring peaks of Castle, Conundrum, Cathedral and Hayden, southeast to more distant but rugged spires in the Sawatch Range — might be considered more breath-taking than the

steady, high-elevation climb. Any number of routes connect the Goodwin-Greene with the Barnard but the easiest course, safest from avalanche, stays off the windy top of the range, maintains elevation and winds cross-country through trees, drafted onto the map as 3.5 miles, 420 feet accumulated elevation gain, 620 feet accumulated elevation loss. Both the Goodwin-Greene and Barnard Huts have reservation limits of four persons minimum for safety, eight maximum. For information on reservations and regulations, see the Markley and Barnard Huts tour (No. 36).

Drive on Colo. 82 to the Maroon Lake/Ashcroft Road west of Aspen, marked by a sign (0.4 mile west of the Castle Creek bridge). Turn south, immediately turn left where the Maroon Lake Road forks right, and continue for 11.7 miles to the Ashcroft Ski Touring Area parking lot on the left side of the road. Overnighters check car keys at Ashcroft Headquarters in the King Cabin, 150 yards up the road at snow closure.

Cross the Castle Creek Valley on a marked public access through the Ashcroft Ski Touring Area, swing right onto the Express Creek Road and begin a southerly traverse up the aspen hillside. Climb steadily after 0.5 mile above picturesque log cabins and false front stores on the valley floor, newly renovated by the Aspen Historical Society, which mark the Ashcroft townsite, a silver mining camp in the 1880's and station for the stage which crossed Taylor Pass via the present ski route. **Proceed quickly across a conspicuous avalanche runout if safe at mile 1.0,** continue the steady climb on the roadbed to scenic vistas of Express Creek Valley, then fork right at 2.1 miles onto the flagged "Touring Hut" trail and contour another 300 yards to a crossing of Express Creek and the Markley Hut.

For the route safest from avalanche, stay in the bottom of the Express Creek Valley rather than follow the roadbed; climb cross-country southeast below avalanche run-outs and eventually enter thicker clumps of spruce at mile 3.6 where an easy climb can be made back to the road. Swing northeast with the valley, stay in the basin on a cross-country course at 4.3 miles where the old Taylor Pass Road, barely visible, turns sharply right toward Taylor Pass, then, **if weather permits,** continue above timberline onto wind-swept, arctic-alpine snowfields and climb at 42°/NE to the first saddle on the right, the 5.1 mile mark and a possible fork between the Bar-

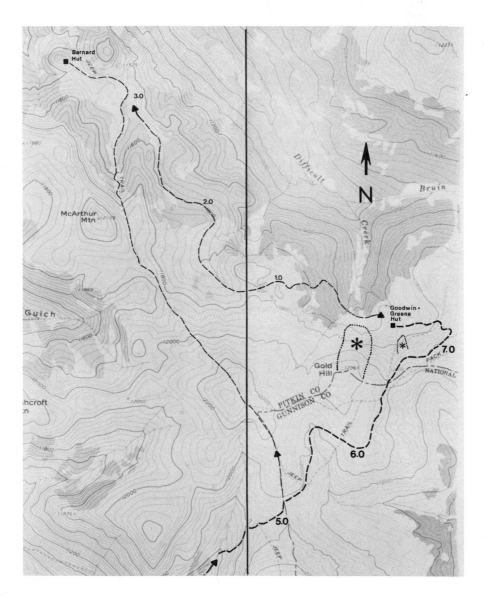

Top of the world

nard Hut and Goodwin-Greene Hut routes. With this climb "the skier moves through vast fields like a dot in a sea of colossal white waves," as aptly described in the *Aspen Trail Guide* by Raymond N. Auger, and the vista, spectacular throughout the tour, gains a new perspective of the snowy Elk Mountains southwest.

For the Goodwin-Greene Hut, contour north from a sign on the saddle, climb southeast above the Bowman Creek bowl to the ridgetop south of Gold Hill at mile 6.1, and bear 8°/NNE to a final saddle at 6.4 miles where the hut shows below (north) on a slight knoll. **Do not drop directly to the hut unless snowpack is very stable** but hook northeast for 0.6 mile then back west over more gentle terrain (see map).

For the Barnard Hut, turn north from the first saddle at mile 5.1 and stay on top of the range, following an up-and-down course. The stunning panorama, sighted from the saddle at mile 5.6, includes: Taylor Peak at 192°/SSW, 14,265-foot Castle Peak at 236°/WSW, and Cathedral Peak at 255°/W in the Elk Mountains, and unnamed, 13,000-foot-plus peaks in the Sawatch Range, highest at 97°/ESE and 88°/ESE. Pass a sign reading "Richmond Hill 3," etc. beyond the saddle, sight the level bench west of McArthur Mtn. at 311°/NW, then drop steeply through wind-crusted snow and scraggly spruce on that bearing and climb toward tree clumps to the right of the bench, the 7.0 mile mark. Drop north into a conspicuous corridor of trees, swing left in front of a forested hill at 8.0 miles, and follow the marked Fall Creek basin west-northwest to the hut, perched atop a knoll of conifers.

38

DIFFICULT CAMPGROUND AND COLORADO HIGHWAY 82

Half-day trips through overnights
Terrain: Easiest
Topographic maps:
  U.S.G.S. Aspen, Colo. 1960
  U.S.G.S. Thimble Rock, Colo. 1960
  U.S.G.S. New York Peak, Colo. 1960
  U.S.G.S. Independence Pass, Colo. 1960
Aspen Ranger District
White River National Forest

The Difficult Campground site, like the upper part of Hunter Creek (No. 39), offers flat and gently-rolling ski terrain quickly accessible from Aspen. With no orienteering or avalanche problems, it makes a delightful "playground" for beginning skiers, families, and anyone who wants an hour or two of smooth gliding, and is used often by ski instructors as a teaching area. The main campground road, figured for the information capsule, carries most of the traffic, often on a well-packed track, but many side roads and powerline cuts loop through the aspen groves and provide more private pathways. One trailcut, used for a slightly longer tour, leads to a bridge over the Roaring Fork River and then climbs gradually southeast up the valley past the Difficult Creek gulch. Although the Difficult Creek Trail which continues on up the gulch has been considered as a possible access to the Barnard Hut (No. 36), it is very steep, difficult to find, crossed by avalanche paths, and therefore not recommended at this time (check with the Aspen Ranger District for changes). In fact, the opinion of the route seems little changed from the one held by two prospectors from Buena Vista who, in the late 1800's, dropped from a main trail on the Taylor Range into the drainage, and fervently sorry that they had, conferred the name onto the creek.

In early November with the first snowfalls and again in about mid-April after the highway has re-opened, skiers drive Colorado 82 to favorite touring areas in the upper Roaring Fork Valley: Independence Pass at 12,093 feet, Lost Man Reservoir Road and Trail north from the switchback above Lost Man Campground, and Lincoln Gulch Road toward Grizzly Reservoir. And then when snow closure at Tagerts Lake goes into effect, usually by early December, the roadbed itself, closed to motorized vehicles, becomes the ski route. Good destinations include Weller Lake Campground near mile 2.0, Grottos Campground at mile 3.1 (figured for the information capsule) and Lost Man Campground at mile 7.8, a good overnight destination. **Be extremely careful of the avalanche danger beyond Lost Man Campground.**

Drive on Colo. 82 through Aspen, turning left (east) at S. Original and E. Cooper and proceeding another 3.7 miles through town into the Roaring Fork Valley to the Difficult Campground turnoff, marked with a large "White River National Forest" sign. For the Difficult Campground tour, park in the large plowed area here. Continue another 1.9 miles for the tour on Colorado Highway 82 to snow closure above Tagerts Lake.

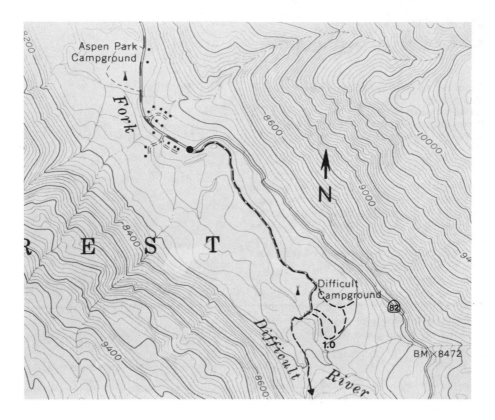

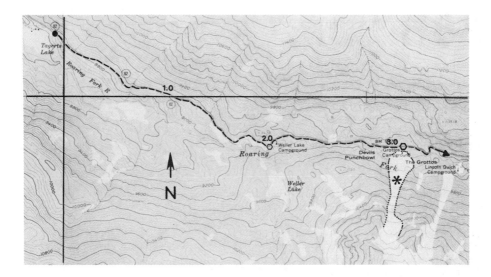

38A DIFFICULT CAMPGROUND

Distance: 1.0 mile/1.6 KM. one way
Skiing time: ½-1 hour one way
Elevation gain: 100 feet/30 M.
Maximum elevation: 8,200 feet/2,499 M.
Season: December through March

Make a fun drop on a curve right to the valley bottom and glide over the snowy roadbed past orange and yellow willows in the riverbed right. Pass a quick glimpse of the white, 12,811-foot New York Peak at 116°/SE, climb then drop very slightly past several Forest Service trailers and the "Difficult Campground" sign, and enter thicker aspen beyond the "Picnic Area." Swing right under a powerline near 1.0 mile and either fork left to the Roaring Fork River bridge or loop right to the starting point.

38B COLORADO HIGHWAY 82

Distance: 3.1 miles/5.0 KM. one way
** (to Grottos Campground Road)**
Skiing time: 1½-2½ hours one way
Elevation gain: 790 feet/241 M.
Maximum elevation: 9,510 feet/2,899 M.
Season: Early December through mid-March

Follow the flat, snow-covered roadbed past these landmarks: a loop through a ravine at 0.8 mile, a rocky roadcut at 2.5 miles, a large basin left at 2.6 miles, and a junction with the Lincoln Creek Road, unmarked on the topo, at 3.1 miles where the rugged Difficult Peak range shows south.

Reflections on winter

39 HUNTER CREEK

Half-day through overnight trips
Terrain: More difficult
Distance: 3.0 miles/4.8 KM. one way
Skiing time: 2-2½ hours one way
Elevation gain: 630 feet/192 M.
Maximum elevation: 8,830 feet/2,691 M.
Season: December through March
Topographic map:
  U.S.G.S. Aspen, Colo. 1960
  U.S.G.S. Thimble Rock, Colo. 1960
Aspen Ranger District
White River National Forest

Three beautiful, snow-blanketed parks, each encircled by stands of open aspen, line the Hunter Creek Valley not more than a mile northeast of Aspen, providing ideal terrain for half-day and one day tours. Although touring tracks often criss-cross the parks and serve as random trails, an even better tour area could be developed easily by the Forest Service with marked — and hence packed-by-use — trails, like those in the Pike, Fairplay, Holy Cross and Leadville Districts. For longer overnight trips a snowy jeep road climbs north from the first park, crosses the Lenado Gulch Trail (the link with the Lenado-Sawmill Park tour), then contours along the north side of Hunter Creek Valley to a mile-long drop through Hunter Flats, and continues east up the valley toward the Williams Mountains. Two exciting possibilities exist for overnight shelters, **in proposal stage only:** the "Hunter Creek cabin," now in one of the lower parks, might be moved to a new site in upper Hunter Creek Valley, or a new cabin might be constructed under the direction of Fred Braun, either of which would be part of the United States Ski Association's Alfred E. Braun Hut System (see No. 36).

The Hunter Creek Trail actually fits within a larger Pitkin County Trail System, established by Aspenites with much collective hard work and with many generous donations for the enjoyment of both citizens and visitors. Thus, a ski tourer may now fly into the Aspen airport at Sardy Field, ski the Rio-Grande Trail for four miles into the middle of town and, from a base at an Aspen lodge, perhaps the historic, convenient Hotel Jerome, explore the Hunter Creek Valley, or even ski all the way to Vail (see No. 40 for the route). However, the private Red Mountain Ranch Homeowners sub-division blocks Forest Service land in Hunter Creek and right-of-way problems complicate the "Grand Scheme." To date there are three access possibilities, none entirely satisfactory: 1) a long, steep, switchbacking climb then drop (and return hike, packing skis) from parking behind the Smuggler Trail Court over Smuggler Mountain via the Smuggler Mountain Road, the legal Forest Service access into Hunter Creek, 2) a short but steep climb from the Water Tower parking lot up the Old Stagecoach Road and across Benedict Bridge, figured for the information capsule and described below, and 3) an easy, smooth-gliding contour from a private Red Mountain road — **a drop-off point only** — to the Upper Hunter Creek Road. For this last access, tourers often pool together for a taxi ride by the Aspen Cab Service Co., telephone 925-2282.

Drive on Colo. 82/East Main to the middle of Aspen, turn left (north) at the Hotel Jerome onto South Mill, then proceed 0.3 mile across the Roaring Fork River to a "Y." Fork left (the right fork leads to an alternate trailhead in about 0.3 mile at the Smuggler Mine Road junction), follow the main road for 0.8 mile across Hunter Creek and continue southeast for another 0.3 mile to a tri-junction — a drop-off point and trailhead but **not** a parking area — where the ski route heads up the gulch via the Old Stagecoach Road. Drive south up the road for 0.1 mile to the Water Tower turnoff where a few parking spaces can usually be found, more if the Water Tower lot has been plowed. Or continue past the Water Tower turnoff onto the Red Mountain Ranch

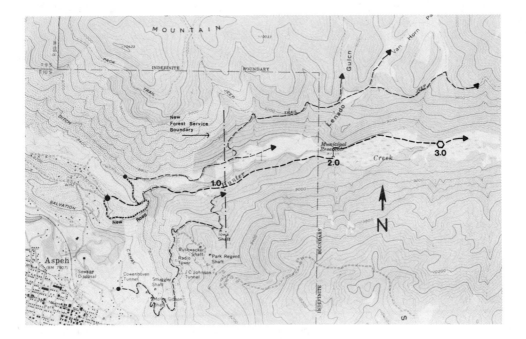

Benedict Bridge bend

Homeowners Assn. road, switchback left and cross the Old Stagecoach Road/ski trail after another 0.5 mile and eventually come to the Upper Hunter Creek Road junction — a drop-off point but again **not** a parking area — 1.0 mile from the Old Stagecoach Road trailhead and 320 feet higher.

Climb steeply on the Old Stagecoach Road up an obvious gulch for 20 yards, turn right through a gate where a private road swings left, soon continue straight where another private road turns right and after 0.1 mile pass the gate chute of the Lars Cutoff summer trail. Intersect a private road at 0.2 mile, continue 25 yards east over the roadbed with a slight drop, then turn left through another chute and contour into the Hunter Creek Valley. Cross the Benedict Bridge at mile 0.4, climb steadily for another 100 yards up the north-facing hillside through shady fir and aspen, and begin gliding on an easier grade into scenic aspen groves. Come to a barbed wire fence at 1.1 miles, the new National Forest boundary; ski through scattered aspen in the first park, cross the Municipal Reservoir Bridge at mile 2.0, and follow a cross-country course through the second park. Pass willows at the far east end and make a slight drop on a snowy road into the third park at 3.0 miles, perhaps a turnback point, where ahead a sharp crag at 94°/ESE and a flat mountainside at 100°/ESE mark the Williams Mountains. Return over the ski tracks, skiing toward a spectacular panorama of peaks, ridges, and bowls in the Elk Mountains, beginning at 210°/SW toward the Maroon Bells and ending at a huge white knob near Capitol Peak at 244°/WSW.

40 SAWMILL PARK

One day trip or overnight
Terrain: Most difficult
Distance: 5.4 miles/8.7 KM. one way
Skiing time: 4½-5½ hours one way
Elevation gain: 2,440 feet/744 M.
Maximum elevation: 11,030 feet/3,362 M.
Season: Late November through early April
Topographic maps:
   U.S.G.S. Aspen, Colo. 1960
   U.S.G.S. Thimble Rock, Colo. 1960
   U.S.G.S. Meredith, Colo. 1970
Aspen Ranger District
White River National Forest

This tour beyond Lenado ventures far from the beaten ski track, first penetrating the cluttered Woody Creek Valley, then climbing steadily to the high saddle of Sawmill Park beneath Porphyry Mountain. Skier and trail-blazer Lars Larsen cleared the route in 1970 for the Forest Service and added high winter blazes where necessary at exactly 90° to the trail to aid in orienteering. Stopping points along the way include the Cliff Creek confluence at 1.0 mile and the Spruce Creek Trail turnoff at 2.0 miles, worthy destinations for intermediate skiers.

The Lenado-Sawmill Park tour, although long, can actually be considered as part of a much longer "Vail to Aspen" ski route, attempted almost every year now by advanced ski mountaineers. The route proceeds from the east end of Lenado over the range to Lenado Gulch and enters Aspen via the Hunter Creek Valley (No. 39). From Sawmill Park at the top of the range the route drops north to Norrie on the Fryingpan River, climbs to a crossing over the Sawatch Range, drops again through the Homestake Creek Valley, and continues from Redcliff to Vail Pass via the Shrine Pass Road (*Northern Colorado Ski Tours* No. 46) or to Vail via the Commando Run (*NCST* No. 48). Avalanche knowledge, route selection and map and compass ability, and winter camping skills are all definite requisites for this adventurous four or five day journey.

Drive on Colo. 82 to the signed Woody Creek Canyon Road northwest of Aspen (over 0.9 mile northwest of the Snowmass Ski Area Road). Turn east, cross the Roaring Fork River, and immediately curve left (north) at a "Y." Proceed another 1.6 miles and turn sharply right just beyond a Sinclair station onto the unmarked Woody Creek Road. Follow this road through the old village of Lenado to snow closure, usually about 8.9 miles from the last junction, and park carefully near the turn-around area.

Ski east from the few cabins and buildings in Lenado, a settlement, now nearly deserted, which was established in the 1880's as a mining camp and later became a center for timber industry. Leave the wide roadbed after about 0.3 mile as it bends sharply left and bear right onto the Woody Creek Trail, marked by a sign if not snow-covered. Pass a steep, rocky slope right, follow the trail through varied dips and climbs, then watch for blazes marking a bend left across Woody Creek at mile 0.9 where dense conifers block the way on the right side. Skirt above the open gulch that fans out from the Cliff Creek drainage, climb steadily beneath the open, south-facing hillside, and re-enter the cool, often snow-laden conifers near the Spruce Creek crossing at mile 2.0, a good stopping point for a shorter tour.

To continue to Sawmill Park, herringbone up a small, steep hill, climb through three short switchbacks, and come to the Spruce Creek Trail junction, marked by signs. Fork left and proceed up the narrow valley: dip left across the creek at 2.2 miles, cross prominent drainages at 2.6 miles, then 3.0 miles, and maintain an easier climb for another mile, gaining a good vista of the Elk Mountains south. Cross open snowfields on the south-facing hillside, begin a more noticeable climb of over-200 feet elevation gain after mile 5.0, then swing right (east) across the Woody Creek drainage and enter the open saddle of Sawmill Park, a good overnight destination. Check speed carefully with snowplow and pole drag on the very steep return.

Sunset over Elk Mountains

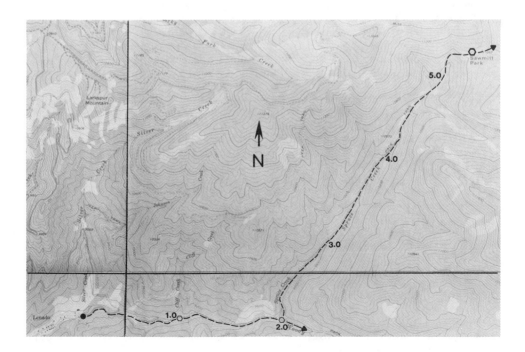

41 BUTTERMILK — SNOWMASS SKI TRAIL

One day trip
Terrain: Most difficult
Distance: 6.5 miles/10.1 KM. one way
Skiing time: 3½-4½ hours one way
Accum. elevation gain: 1,070 feet/326 M.
Accum. elevation loss: 1,510 feet/460 M.
Maximum elevation: 9,380 feet/2,859 M.
Season: Late November through early April
Topographic map:
   U.S.G.S. Highland Peak, Colo. 1960
Aspen Ranger District
White River National Forest

This route, known also as the Brush Creek Trail and the Government Trail, begins near the base of the West Buttermilk Ski Area amid the hurly-burly of alpine skiers but then escapes quickly into quiet and scenic woods. It proceeds on a varied course of short climbs, easy-gliding flats, and rolling drops, contouring the northern reaches of Burnt Mountain, and ends on a long downhill among alpine skiers again at the Snowmass Ski Area. A favorite among Aspen locals due to its proximity to town, the tour route has been re-cut and blazed in recent years and often has a well-broken track. Variations include 1) skiing from Snowmass Ski Area to Buttermilk, the "reverse" direction with substantially more climb than drop, 2) skiing from either Buttermilk or Snowmass to mid-point at Kelly's Park and back which simplifies transportation, or 3) skiing the entire distance and back in one day, done by advanced skiers when the track has set up or in spring on the hard crust.

In Snowmass, down the valley from the Buttermilk-Snowmass Trail end point at the ski area complex, another popular ski touring area has been established, using the rolling hills around the Snowmass Country Club golf course. With loop trails that are packed and machine-set with tracks, this area — free to the public — attracts beginners and racers, ski touring classes and lone individuals on short but quiet tours. For more information, contact the Snowmass Ski Touring Center at (303) 923-4012.

Although thousands of recreational skiers, both alpine and nordic, now come to Aspen each year for a pleasure vacation, this area —

the same valleys and meadows along the Buttermilk-Snowmass Trail, in fact — was skied first out of necessity, long before the establishment of ski lifts and condominiums. Mrs. Lysle Burnett Lawson, now of Rifle, who grew up on the old Burke Ranch below the Snowmass Ski Area, remembers skiing as a necessary part of running a cattle ranch. "The skis had straps to hold on the cowboy boots and Mother would sew old overall legs into "skins" for climbing. If the cattle didn't come in, then we would have to ski to look for strays. My brothers didn't think much of it," she adds, summing up those early-day efforts.

Drive on Colo. 82 to the Buttermilk Ski Area turnoff northwest of Aspen (1.4 miles northwest of the Castle Creek bridge.) Turn west, pass the ski area parking zone, and proceed straight onto the Buttermilk West Road, marked by a sign. Eventually stay left where a lower road marked "Ambulance Entrance" proceeds to the bottom of Lift 3, and come to the private Buttermilk West parking lot at the road's end, a total of 3.2 miles from Colo. 82. Arrange for a car pick-up and meeting place at the Snowmass Ski Area. Note: Parking privileges in the private ski area lots are available by courtesy of the ski areas, subject to change.

Contour carefully west across the West Buttermilk alpine slope beneath Lift 3, make a steady climb beyond the fourth lift tower, and fork right onto an obvious roadcut through aspen, soon coming to a vista of snow-capped Burnt Mountain at 222°/SW. Climb steadily across several drainages, pass through an open metal gate and above cabin ruins, then bend left above the Owl Creek drainage at mile 0.6 and curve right around an open park, unmarked on the topo. Contour above two cabins and the obvious Whites lakebed after 1.5 miles, cross into National Forest property at mile 1.7 and ski through thick pine to an easy downhill, ending near East Fork Spring Creek at 2.3 miles. Make another rolling drop to a crossing of West Fork Spring Creek after 3.0 miles and break onto the wide snowfields of Kelly Park at mile 3.2, a possible lunch spot and turn-back point. Contour to a crossing of East Fork Creek at mile 4.1, cross two more branches at miles 4.2 and 4.4, then pass the summer trail (left), follow blazes on a climb to a ridgetop and end with a rolling, 1.6 mile descent (see map).

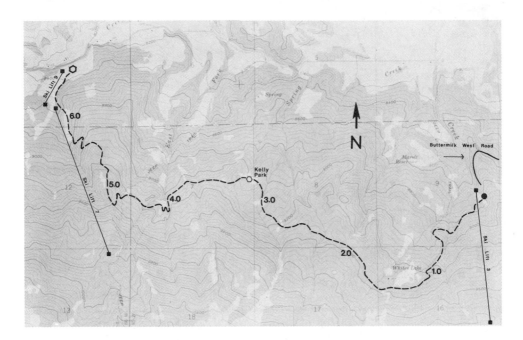

Heading home

42 HAY PARK TRAIL

One day trip or overnight
Terrain: Most difficult
Distance: 6.9 miles/11.1 KM. one way
Skiing time: 5½-6 hours one way
Accum. elevation gain: 2,145 feet/654 M.
Accum. elevation loss: 425 feet/130 M.
Maximum elevation: 9,700 feet/2,957 M.
Season: Mid-December through early April
Topographic maps:
  U.S.G.S. Basalt, Colo. 1961
  U.S.G.S. Capitol Peak, Colo. 1960
Aspen Ranger District
White River National Forest

Solitude is the chief virtue of the Hay Park Trail, a quiet, scenic tour route which forks west after 1.4 miles off the beaten track of the Williams Lake Trail (No. 43). Marked with an assortment of blazes, tin tabs, and orange arrows, it climbs a steep, aspen hillside on a public right-of-way through private property, and comes to a splendid lookout of twin-topped Mount Sopris at mile 2.4, a satisfying stopping point. For a longer tour, the trail can be followed all the way to Hay Park at the top of the range, as figured in the information capsule, and then continued down the west side to the Dinkle and Thomas Lakes trails (No. 44). This extended trip, possible in mid-winter as an overnight or in spring as a long, one-day trip over the fast snowcrust, penetrates deep thickets of spruce and links many snowy clearings (not shown on the topo), unsurpassed terrain for ski touring.

Drive on Colo. 82 to the old town of Snowmass, 8.7 miles northwest of the Snowmass-At-Aspen Ski Area turnoff. Turn south at the gas station onto the Snowmass Creek Road, fork right in 1.8 miles onto the Capitol Creek Road where a sign reads "Capitol Creek Administrative Site 8," etc., and stay right past the Saint Benedict's Monastery turnoff after 5.3 miles. Continue to the end of the plowed road which is usually another 1.5 miles from the Monastery turnoff, a total distance of 6.8 miles from Colo. 82. Park carefully along the roadside.

Ski southwest from snow closure over the wide roadbed, cross Little Elk Creek near a corral and ranch buildings after 0.9 mile, and continue over a slight hill and along a willow basin to the Hay Park Trail turnoff at mile 1.4, opposite a sign reading "3 Capitol

Creek/Snowmass 10." Fork right through a metal gate, bear to the right of the main clump of spruce in the basin, and climb gradually west through the open snowfields, keeping left of the fence line. On the horizon at 6°/NNE the long, blue-and-white range of Red Table Mountain can be seen, appearing as a giant caterpillar with legs of ravines and ridges. Pass a sign identifying "Hay Park Trail" just inside the first aspen (Capitol Creek Guard Station has been torn down), begin a steep climb west through open aspen, and break into a meadow near mile 2.1, again with a panoramic view of white peaks and blue ranges.

Pick up the trail 20 yards from the fence line, soon ski over a ditch and through a gate, and continue to the ridgetop at mile 2.4 where an old sign reads "7 Dinkle Lake/4 Hay Park," a good stopping point. Here the two snowy, wind-chiseled peaks of Sopris and West Sopris, both at 12,953 feet, loom into the skyline, visible on a 264°/W bearing over five miles away. To continue to Hay Park, follow the trail markers west on a steep, 20 yard drop and intercept a conspicuous jeep trail. Contour southwest through a double drainage at mile 3.2, ski across open snowfields and cross through a fence after 3.7 miles, then follow the "Foot and Horseback" trail across more meadows, none marked on the topo. Enter stands of stately spruce and fir, often laden with snow, and begin bearing northwest, then north through open parks. Here the trail becomes hard to follow (scheduled for remarking possibly in 1977). Using topo map and compass, negotiate the final two miles and 200 feet elevation gain to the broad, open saddle of Hay Park.

Mount Sopris

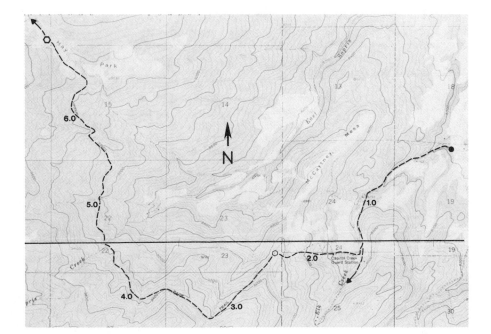

43 WILLIAMS LAKE TRAIL

One day trip or overnight
Terrain: More difficult to most difficult
Distance: 6.0 miles/9.7 KM. one way
Skiing time: 5-5½ hours one way
Elevation gain: 2,835 feet/864 M.
Maximum elevation: 10,815 feet/3,296 M.
Season: Mid-December through early April
Topographic maps:
  U.S.G.S. Basalt, Colo. 1961
  U.S.G.S. Capitol Peak, Colo. 1960
Aspen Ranger District
White River National Forest

Blanketed with deep snow or wind-blown to a tawny brown, blazing with sunlight or veiled in thick clouds, the massive rock summit of Capitol Peak and the surrounding alpine mountains of the Elk Range always create a powerful spectacle in winter. This view, seen first from the Williams Lake Trail after 3.3 miles and 1,440 feet of elevation gain, is the drawing card which attracts a number of ski tourers to the area every weekend and keeps the trail well-broken.

The tour route begins near a ranch house on an unplowed country road, the first place to lose snow cover in spring, and provides access also to the rancher who travels by snowmobile to feed his cattle and to others who ski to their cabins at mile 2.2. After passing the Hay Park Trail turnoff (No. 42) at mile 1.4, the route climbs more steeply, following the Little Elk Creek valley, then the ridgeline to the lookout. With provisions for an overnight camp or with the fast, early-morning crust in spring, the tour can be continued to Hardscrabble Lake or, as figured in the information capsule, to Williams Lake, an uphill extension with different perspectives of the Elk Mountains vista. Necessary technique for the return trip — a superb run with powder snow — include an effective snowplow and pole drag.

Henry Gannett, leader of the topographic and geographic division of Hayden's Geological Survey, or his geographer, W.D. Whitney, named Capitol Peak, "for its dome-like crest," according to Len Shoemaker in *Roar-*

ing Fork Valley. The peak had an interesting growing period. First estimated at 13,997 feet by the Hayden Survey, it was given an extra three feet by a later survey to make it one of Colorado's Fourteeners, and eventually reassessed by a modern survey to its present height of 14,130 feet, 30th highest in the state.

Drive on Colo. 82 to the old town of Snowmass, 8.7 miles northwest of the Snowmass-At-Aspen Ski Area turnoff. Turn south at the gas station onto the Snowmass Creek Road, fork right in 1.8 miles onto the Capitol Creek Road where a sign reads "Capitol Creek Administrative Site 8," etc., and stay right past the Saint Benedict's Monastery turnoff after 5.3 miles. Continue to the end of the plowed road which is usually another 1.5 miles from the Monastery turnoff, a total distance of 6.8 miles from Colo. 82. Park carefully along the roadside.

Glide southwest on the snowy roadbed through groves of aspen and conifers and past open meadows. Swing left across Little Elk Creek near a corral and ranch buildings at mile 0.9, make a short climb over the hillside left and proceed straight at 1.4 miles where the Hay Park Trail forks right through a gate. Continue the gradual climb past several cabins across Little Elk Creek after 2.2 miles, soon cross then re-cross a drainageway, and climb steadily to a westerly bearing, passing the White River National Forest boundary sign at mile 2.7. Traverse a hillside of aspen above an open meadow right, gaining a view behind of the distant Red Table Mountain with its deep red, maroon, and blue colors. Then enter thicker aspen and make the steep climb to the lookout at 3.3 miles, a good lunch stop and turning back point. In the foreground the treeless knob of Haystack Mountain rises at 156°/S from a forested range left, and beyond, the alpine summit of Capitol Peak shows, dominating the skyline at 170°/S. A scalloped ridge leads right to a 12,878-foot peak at 180°/SSW, and on the horizon farther right, a 12,176-foot peak stands out at 230°/WSW between glacial cirques, both unnamed peaks in the Elk Mountains.

For a longer tour, follow the snowy jeep road west past these landmarks: a meadow with a Forest Service marker at 3.7 miles, a ridgetop climb to another lookout above a point at 4.3 miles, a climb through thick fir to the Hardscrabble Lake turnoff at 4.5 miles, and a climb to Williams Lake at 6.0 miles.

Family fun

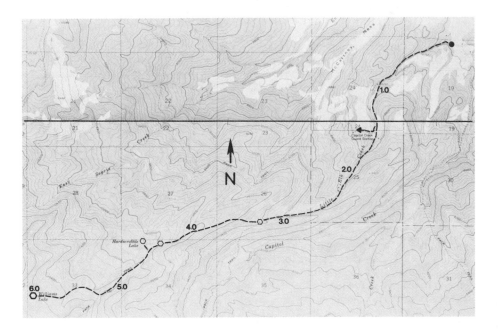

44 DINKLE AND THOMAS LAKES

One day trips or overnights
Terrain: More difficult
Topographic maps:
  U.S.G.S. Basalt, Colo. 1961
  U.S.G.S. Mount Sopris, Colo. 1961
Sopris Ranger District
White River National Forest

In 1860 "Captain" Richard Sopris, for whom the 12,953-foot Mt. Sopris is named, led an expedition of gold seekers into the central Colorado mountains. The group journeyed along the Arkansas River between the Mosquito and Sawatch Ranges, crossed over Tennessee Pass and followed the Eagle River down to its confluence with the Colorado River. Then, finding their way blocked by the narrow, steep Glenwood Canyon, they turned south over Cottonwood Pass where the majestic, snow-capped summit of Mt. Sopris caught the Captain's eye. Vowing to the others that he intended to ride his mule Jerry to the top of that mountain, Sopris set out from camp for his goal. After a long climb up the steep slopes, Sopris and Jerry found the way blocked by a huge snowdrift. Sopris urged and pleaded, then whipped and kicked but Jerry, belly-deep in snow, lay down and refused to budge, leaving the Captain with a long walk down the mountain. Sopris believed that the mule was seriously injured and was quite remorseful about losing him in such a manner. The group proceeded some 25 more miles on down the Roaring Fork River and stopped at the hot springs of present-day Glenwood Springs. That evening all were surprised and overjoyed when Jerry the mule hee-hawed into camp, looking suspiciously healthy after his ordeal.

Drive on Colo. 82 to the Fryingpan River bridge south of Basalt, turn south just before the west end of the bridge onto the road to Emma and immediately cross the Roaring Fork River. Turn right (west), curve left (south) across the railroad tracks at Emma where another road forks right, and turn right again in another 1.0 mile. Continue another 4.3 miles to the end of the plowed road near a ranch house, almost 7.0 miles from Colo. 82, and park in an out-of-the-way spot along the roadside.

White tailed Ptarmigan

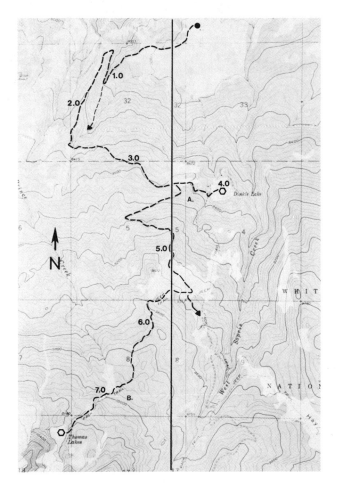

44A  DINKLE LAKE

44B THOMAS LAKE

Distance: 4.0 miles/6.4 KM. one way
Skiing time: 3-3½ hours one way
Accum. elevation gain: 1,040 feet/317 M.
Accum. elevation loss: 140 feet/43 M.
Maximum elevation: 8,640 feet/2,633 M.
Season: Mid-December through late April

Distance: 7.6 miles/12.2 KM. one way
Skiing time: 5-5½ hours one way
Elevation gain: 2,540 feet/774 M.
Maximum elevation: 10,200 feet/3,109 M.
Season: Early December through mid-April

With a splendid view of the Mt. Sopris range from the start, the popular tour to Dinkle and Thomas Lakes begins on a low-elevation road where snow cover varies from year to year, especially in December. After 1.1 miles either switchback right then bend left to a ridgetop course on the road or follow a shortcut at 181°/SSW up a drainage of scrub oak and aspen. Bend east on the road at 2.4 miles, climb through aspen to a cattle guard at 3.0 miles, the National Forest boundary. Bend right then left on a gradual climb and break onto an open knoll at mile 3.5. Here signs marks the turnoffs right to ''Thomas Lake 3/Hay Park 3'' while the route marked ''Dinkle Lake ½'' proceeds east. Bend right after another 300 yards near trees and make an easy, winding drop to the open Dinkle lakebed at 4.0 miles, a good lunch and camp spot.

Turn south from the signpost on the open knoll at 3.5 miles, cross-country through aspen and scrub oak for 75 yards until hitting the roadcut, then turn right and proceed through a blow-down into thick spruce and fir. Switchback left after 4.1 miles and climb steadily, gaining a good view of the open snowfield near the start and of distant Sawatch Peaks northeast. Fork right at a sign reading ''Thomas Lake 2'' at 5.3 miles where the road stays left to Hay Park, an excellent alternate route (see No. 42). Ski cross-country as the trail becomes faint; bear toward the rugged, cirque-topped Mount Sopris summit and continue up Prince Creek to Thomas Lake at 7.6 miles. **Be very careful of avalanches beyond.**

45 McCLURE PASS

One day trip
Terrain: Easiest
Distance: 3.2 miles/5.1 KM. one way
Skiing time: 2-2½ hours one way
Accum. elevation gain: 975 feet/297 M.
Accum. elevation loss: 80 feet/24 M.
Maximum elevation: 9,660 feet/2,944 M.
Season: Late November through April
Topographic maps:
  U.S.G.S. Placita, Colo. 1963
  U.S.G.S. Chair Mountain, Colo. 1963
Paonia Ranger District
Gunnison National Forest

The well-traveled tour south from McClure Pass follows a recently constructed road — not shown on the 1963 topos but drafted onto the map photo — which loops high above the Crystal River Valley and then contours along the west side of the mountain range to private property. Aspens and conifers shelter the roadbed from wind for much of the way, an easy uphill grade encourages long glides, and avalanche and orienteering problems are minimal, conditions which create an ideal tour for all ages and abilities. Although the road can be toured as far as the private land at 4.5 miles, shorter destinations include an open park near the Ragged Mountain Trail turnoff at 2.2 miles, a high mountain meadow with a good vista at 3.2 miles, and the high ridge at 4.2 miles. Another fun route, one of many cross-country possibilities, leaves the roadbed after 2.5 miles, loops north through a slight saddle, and makes a long, downhill traverse through conifer and aspen clumps until intercepting the roadbed again (see map). Snowmobiles are allowed currently on the new roadbed but a motor closure is being considered. For information, contact the Paonia Ranger District, Paonia, CO 81428, telephone (303) 527-4131.

Drive on Colo. 133 to the top of McClure Pass south of Carbondale and northeast of Paonia, 6.7 miles east of the "West Muddy Creek" turnoff. Find parking along the south side of the highway.

Pass through a metal gate on the south side of McClure Pass and begin skiing east-southeast over the obvious, snow-covered road. Curve right above the winding curves of the Colo. 133 highway and the deep Crystal River Valley, soon stay right where an old roadbed turns left, and pass views of the scarp ridge and sharp, snow-capped peak and forested knobs that comprise the Elk Mountain Range east-southeast. Ski by an old summer trail turnoff, marked "502," at mile 0.4, drop and climb through a slight ravine, then climb gradually through aspen and farther on, through spruce and fir, and cross several small tributaries of Lee Creek. Bend south after 1.6 miles on the serene, aspen-lined roadbed and break into a spacious park at mile 2.2, a possible turn-back point, where the view extends southwest to forested mountainsides beyond the Muddy Creek Valley.

Bend east through deer-scared aspen, passing more open meadows right and come to another sign reading "502" at 2.5 miles where a cross-country loop can be made toward the saddle to the north. Continuing on the roadbed, make a slow arc right above the headwaters of Chair Creek and enter an open park at 3.2 miles, another good tour destination. Here a beautiful, green and white panorama stretches across the skyline with the northern, 11,866-foot summit and sharp ridge of Chair Mountain at 152°/SSE, Pilot Knob beyond Muddy Creek at 215°/SW, and the more gentle contours of Sheep Mountain at 242°/WSW. The roadbed continues south through the open park, enters a corridor of trees where snow is noticeably deeper, then climbs gradually to the ridgetop at 3.5 miles and crosses an east-west range at 4.1 miles, another stopping point with a closer view of the lofty Chair Mountain Range south.

Midwinter's lunch

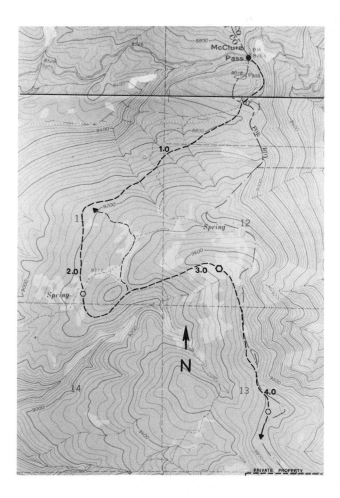

46 CLEAR FORK TRAIL

One day trip
Terrain: Easiest
Distance: 3.4 miles/5.5 KM. one way
Skiing time: 2-2½ hours one way
Elevation gain: 390 feet/119 M.
Maximum elevation: 7,640 feet/2,329 M.
Season: Mid-December through March
Topographic maps:
　U.S.G.S. Bull Mountain, Colo. 1963
　U.S.G.S. Elk Knob, Colo. 1963
Paonia Ranger District
Gunnison National Forest

On busy winter weekends when tour groups crowd the McClure Pass area (No. 45), the snow on the nearby East Muddy Creek Road and Clear Fork Trail often remains smooth and unbroken, an enticing alternative to the tourer who seeks solitude. This trip stays in foothills country, the relatively low Transition Life Zone, which imparts a refreshing different mood to the tour. Silver-gray cottonwoods, a very rare tree on a Colorado tour route, mingle with stately blue spruce along the valley and scrub oak cover the southfacing hillsides. The tracks of mule deer, coyotes, rabbits, sometimes even elk, bobcats, and bear criss-cross the snowfields, and with a little stealth and quiet plus some luck these animals might be spotted, especially toward late afternoon and evening.

The tour begins from snow closure on the Muddy Creek Road/Forest Service 265, usually near the Colo. 133 junction in winter and closer to the Henderson Creek and Sylvan Lodge area in spring, and proceeds north through easy, near-level terrain toward the Clear Fork Valley. Destinations depend only on the starting point and amount of time for the tour but definite goals to shoot for include the Little Muddy Creek confluence at 1.9 miles (figured from the Sylvan Lodge turnoff), the Gooseberry Trail junction, computed for the information capsule, and, the long snowfield of Clear Fork Park at 10.5 miles, highly recommended for an overnight trip. The route as described below stays on an old, public stage road through private property. However, right-of-way is unclear and the Forest Service is currently negotiating for a

horse-and-foot trail access. Contact the Paonia Ranger District, Paonia, CO 81428, telephone (303) 527-4131 for recent developments.

Drive on Colo. 133 north from Paonia Reservoir for 7.8 miles to the road junction marked "National Forest Access/West Muddy Creek/Collbran 50," 6.7 miles west of McClure Pass. Turn west, proceed another 4.6 miles to the Sylvan Lodge or as close to the lodge as road conditions safely permit, and find parking along the roadside. By 1982 or so the road may possibly be plowed into Henderson Park, two miles west of the Sylvan Lodge.

Follow the East Muddy Creek Road northwest until reaching the Sylvan Lodge turnoff, marked by a sign, 0.2 miles beyond the Little Henderson Creek bridge. Turn north through the barbed wire fence and glide over the roadbed past spruce and cottonwood trees which line East Muddy Creek (right). Cross the creekbed after 0.4 mile, then ski cross-country along the left side of a meadow where the roadbed becomes obscure, passing a view of the spectacular ravine-and-ridge formation called The Raggeds at 133°/SE over 10 miles away, and the blue, jagged summit of Marcellina Mountain beyond the Dark Canyon (No. 47) at 130°/SE. Pick up the roadbed after 0.9 mile at the upper end of the meadow, ski in and out of blue spruce and aspen over gently-rolling terrain, and soon come to a viewpoint of a blue ridge and four, white amphitheaters, highest near East Beckwith Mountain — the north end of the West Elk Wilderness Area — at 137°/SSE.

Pass through another barbed wire fence at 1.6 miles (the north boundary of Section 3), contour along a hillside past the Clear Fork Creek confluence and gaging station at 1.9 miles, and climb to a good view of the Little Muddy Creek basin, a possible stopping point. To continue into the Clear Fork Valley, fork left through sage at mile 2.1 where another road climbs right, cross Coal Creek in several hundred more yards, then glide through the open hillside to Dead Horse Creek in mile 2.8, and after crossing and re-crossing Clear Fork Creek, come to the Gooseberry Creek drainage at 3.4 miles, another good turn-back point. For longer tours, continue north up the more narrow and secluded valley, passing the many-fingered tributaries of Clear Fork Creek as shown on the topo.

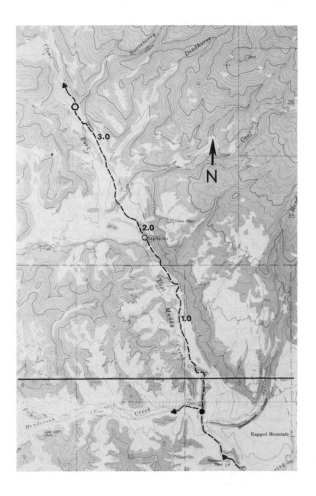

Rabbit tracks

47 DARK CANYON

One day trip or overnight
Terrain: Easiest to more difficult
Distance: 3.7 miles/6.0 KM. one way
Skiing time: 2-2½ hours one way
Elevation gain: 420 feet/128 M.
Maximum elevation: 7,180 feet/2,188 M.
Season: Mid-December through early April
Topographic maps:
   U.S.G.S. Paonia Reservoir, Colo. 1964
   U.S.G.S. Marcellina Mtn., Colo. 1961
Paonia Ranger District
Gunnison National Forest

Dark Canyon ... Bear Gulch ... Lightning Ridge...Hell Creek... Devils Stairway. From a look only at the place names on the Marcellina Mtn. topo, it would appear that the terrain west of the Ruby Range and east of Paonia Reservoir is rough and wild. The area is indeed a rugged and pristine part of the Gunnison National Forest, soon to be considered for Wilderness Area designation, which few Coloradoans know about. Far from major population centers and much less publicized than other areas of wilderness, it offers the advanced ski tourer and winter camper an adventurous escape from the maddening crowd. The tour begins near the Erickson Springs Campground on Anthracite Creek with a beautiful view of The Raggeds, then follows the snow-packed creekbed east through the high, narrow walls of the Dark Canyon, an exceptionally scenic but much colder and more shaded canyon than the one which rises above East Rifle Creek (No. 52). **However, one note of caution: The canyon floor makes a no-escape trap for slides which spill out of unseen snow caches on the mountainside above. Therefore, never venture into this area after periods of wind and snow when avalanche danger is high.** The tour route reaches the confluence of Middle Anthracite and Ruby Anthracite Creeks after 3.7 miles, the turn-back point figured for the information capsule, but extended trips can be attempted along either drainage, possibly as far as the steep, arctic-alpine summits of the

Ruby Range west of the Crested Butte tours at Lily Lake and Floresta (No. 29) and at Lake Irwin (No. 30).

Drive on Colo. 133 beyond the south end of Paonia Reservoir to the turnoff marked ''Paonia Reservoir/Redstone/Crested Butte.'' Turn east across the North Fork Gunnison River, stay left where the Coal Creek Road/No. 709 forks right after 1.6 miles, then proceed past the Dark Canyon summer trailhead to the Anthracite Creek bridge at 6.1 miles and find off-the-road parking in another hundred yards where the road bends.

Drop past the large steel bridge onto the Anthracite creekbed and ski northeast over wide snowfields and around black water pockets. Near the start the rock-ribbed range called The Raggeds, one of central Colorado's most beautiful formations, shows on the skyline from 338°/N to 40°/NE, blazing white with snow above the drier, brown foreground range. Continue over the creekbed or follow the summer trail which contours along the north side, passing through an interesting water habitat where cottonwood trees line the valley, raccoon tracks sometimes show in the snow, and in spring, belted kingfishers and dippers fly along the creek. Pass private houses (left) after 0.3 mile, wind past sedimentary rock outcroppings to the canyon mouth at mile 1.2, then ski by rock walls left — colored with oranges, grays, slate black, moss green from the lichen and looking like rough, cracked concrete — and pass smooth, often snow-dusted rock walls right.

If avalanche conditions are low, ski quickly and singly past fan-shaped run-outs near 1.8 and 1.9 miles; bend right to an east-southeast bearing, enter a shadier, colder part of the canyon, and skirt a large talus field (left) after 2.3 miles. Come to the first view of the Ruby Range in several more yards where 12,646-foot Afley Peak gleams above the dark end of the canyon at 101°/ESE. Pass an obvious tributary (right) at mile 2.9, bend right again in several more hundred yards, passing Bear Gulch (left), then curve left at another tributary at 3.3. miles and follow the flat creekbed past talus fields toward the magnificent summits of Hancock and Oh-be-Joyful Peak at 90°/ESE in the Ruby Range. After 3.7 miles break onto an open snowfield which leads right (south) to the deep canyon of Ruby Anthracite Creek, a good turnback point for a long, one-day tour.

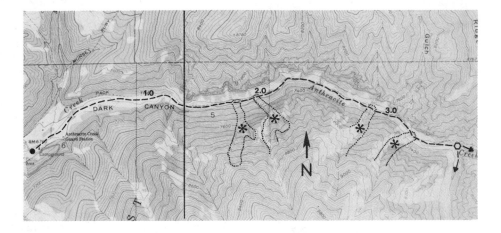

Spring thaw along Anthracite Creek

48 MARION GULCH

One day trip
Terrain: More difficult
Distance: 8.7 miles/14.0 KM. one way
Skiing time: 3½-4½ hours one way
Accum. elevation gain: 1,475 feet/450 M.
Accum. elevation loss: 1,440 feet/439 M.
Maximum elevation: 9,120 feet/2,780 M.
Season: Early December through late March
Topographic map:
U.S.G.S. Stony Ridge, Colo. 1963
Sopris Ranger District
White River National Forest

The Marion Gulch tour, southwest of Carbondale, crosses the open snowfields of Jerome Park and climbs gradually west up the other side of the range from Babbish Gulch (No. 49) and Beaver Creek (No. 50). By contouring northwest along the top of the range for 1½-2 miles, the tour can easily be linked to these other drainages and then ended with a zipping descent to either the Sunlight Ski Area or Fourmile Park. Another well-used return route, figured for the information capsule and described below, turns south near the range top into the Yank Creek drainage and makes a long, gradual drop to a pick-up point above the Thompson Creek Mine. For this return, keep in mind that the drive access crosses through the private, operating mine area, owned by the Anshutz Coal Corporation. Be alert for the mine trucks while driving and park in an out-of-the-way spot near road closure.

Still another tour option — used sometimes as a training course by the Rocky Mountain School in Carbondale and then broken with a hard track — forks left at 0.8 mile near the Marion Cemetery onto an old roadbed and contours south above Jerome Park. The tour route climbs to lookout points of the beautiful Elk Mountains near Capitol Peak southeast and of the Huntsman Ridge south, passes coke ovens (marked on the topo) which served the American steel effort during World War I, and finishes with an exciting descent to a pick-up point on the road. Despite the relatively low 8,300-foot maximum elevation, this tour route receives heavy snowfall, as do the Babbish Gulch (No. 49) and Beaver Creek and Fourmile Park (No. 50) tours. Even when spring weather prevails

in Carbondale, go prepared for winter here.

Drive on Colo. 133 toward Carbondale and turn right (west) where a main turnoff, marked "Carbondale Business District," turns left. Proceed another 0.8 mile on a curve right toward Red Hill, turn left onto "108 Road" where "106 Road" continues ahead to the Rocky Mountain School, then follow the main road past the Dry Park Road at 4.0 miles and come to the Marion Gulch Road turnoff, 6.3 miles from Colo. 133. Park along the roadside here or, if the Marion Gulch roadbed is open, turn right (west) and continue to snow closure. To get to the "training course" pick-up point or to the Thompson Creek Mine pick-up point, drive south from the Marion Gulch Road, proceeding 2.7 miles to the junction with the training course road and 4.3 miles to the mine. Follow the main road another 0.7 mile through the mine area and stay left to a small parking spot where the road loops right to a green building.

Ski west over the Marion Gulch roadbed on a slight climb and come to a junction after 0.8 mile: one road — the "training course" — forks left on a climb and the other road forks right past the Marion Cemetery and through an aspen grove and ravine to another road fork at 0.9 mile, a possible starting point in early winter and late spring when the road below is passable. Take the left fork into Marion Gulch, continue on a rolling course through exquisite white aspen, then cross through a barbed wire fence after 1.6 miles and drop left to a creek crossing. Soon re-cross the creek, climb through aspen, scrub oak and occasional cedar, and follow the route — now trail-size — on a climb above an open park at mile 2.4. Pass to the right then left side of a slight ridge on a climb which brings into view the cliff wall of Huntsman Ridge, highest at the 11,786-foot point of Huntsman Mountain at 171°/S, and other snowy peaks east. Arc left after 2.8 miles across a ravine (left) and break into an open ridgetop park at mile 3.0, a good turnback point for a short, one-day tour.

Contour around the side of a protruding ridge at 3.1 miles, passing through an open gate. Pass a roadbed (right) which leads northwest to Babbish Gulch and Beaver Creek, coast southwest on a long, fun descent to Yank Creek at mile 4.0, then pick up the jeep road which stays right of Yank and North Thompson Creek all the way to the Thompson Creek Mine pick-up at mile 8.7.

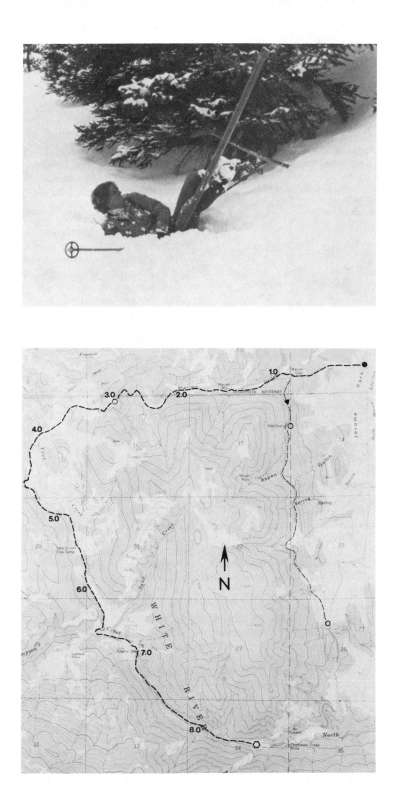

49 BABBISH GULCH

Half-day and one day trips
Terrain: More difficult
Distance: 2.1 miles/3.4 KM. one way
Skiing time: 1½ hours one way
Elevation gain: 850 feet/259 M.
Maximum elevation: 8,970 feet/2,734 M.
Season: Early December through late March
Topographic map:
  U.S.G.S. Cattle Creek, Colo. 1961
Sopris Ranger District
White River National Forest

The Babbish Gulch tour begins near the base of the Sunlight Ski Area and follows the Old Fourmile Creek roadbed west onto the narrow gulch floor, a route very much like the well-traveled Guller Creek Loop near the Copper Mountain Ski Area (*Northern Colorado Ski Tours* No. 41). This tour offers skiing variety for all people and all seasons: Cross-country purists will enjoy climbing through the attractive aspen and conifer groves along the gulch bottom and skiing the open basin and hillsides near mile 2.1, a good lunch and turn-back point. The alpine-nordic hybrids can ride the Sunlight Ski Area chairlift to the top of Compass Point (single ride ticket — $3), ski the fast, packed Ute Trail for about 500 yards to a slight knoll, then turn west into the aspen and make a contouring drop to Babbish Gulch. And ski mountaineers with an urge to climb might want to attempt the 10,079-foot Williams Peak west of Babbish Gulch, a trip of exceptionally good skiing after a new powder snowfall but not recommended during windy weather. Other popular downhill routes from the Compass Point summit exit through Freeman Creek, Marion Gulch and Yank Creek (No. 48), and Beaver Creek (No. 50) (see map). **Obtain weather information and leave a route plan with the Sunlight Ski Area ski patrol before starting out, telephone (303) 945-7491.**

Drive on Colo. 82 to the south end of Glenwood Springs, turn right onto Grand Ave. and proceed 0.3 mile, then cross a bridge, turn left onto "117 Rd." and continue 1.5 miles to "116 Rd." Turn right (south) and follow this main road for 8.9 miles toward the Sunlight Ski Area. Continue straight where the Fourmile Creek Road forks right, loop left across Fourmile Creek in another 0.6 mile and park in a small open area on the right or park several hundred yards down the road in the ski area parking lot.

Begin skiing west over the Old Fourmile Creek Road or along the base of the Sunlight Ski Area. Pass through scenic aspen groves, stay left around a private cabin at mile 0.7, then curve left (south) into the bottom of the gulch and climb gradually on a cross-country course. Enter thick aspen, conifers and willows on a steeper climb after 1.1 miles and break into a small clearing in another 200 yards where a cross-country route turns left (east), contours to the top of an old chairlift and then drops to the Sunlight Ski Area base over a maintenance road or down the Ute ski run, making an alternate return route. Continue the southerly cross-country climb, skiing through aspen along the hillside when the gulch bottom becomes too cluttered with willows. Pass a series of beaver dams in the creekbed and after 1.8 miles ski by the ruins of an old cabin west of the creek, sometimes buried by snow, which served in earlier days as the office for the timber operation in Babbish Gulch. Continue into a wide, serene park at mile 2.0, a good end point for the tour, where the panorama includes Williams Peak at 271°/WNW, the saddle destination at 236°/WSW for the climb to Williams Peak, the Babbish Gulch headwall south and the Ute ski run at 114°/SE.

To climb over the headwall for access into the other drainages, bear 194°/SSW from the park toward the low point on the skyline. Weave through islands of aspen on a steady climb for another 0.5 mile. **Stay out of the narrow gulches which drop from the headwall and away from the open, corniced ridges.** Keep in trees on a slight ridge as much as possible to minimize avalanche danger and sidestep and herringbone up the final, very steep wall. From the headwall top the tour may be continued into Beaver Creek by bearing across a wide snowfield toward another low point on the skyline at 222°/WSW. The Yank Creek access proceeds due south beyond a barbed wire fence and into a willow-filled basin, and the Freeman Creek and Marion Gulch access curves southeast and begins a contour toward the ridge which connects summits "9698" and "9437."

Threading the aspen

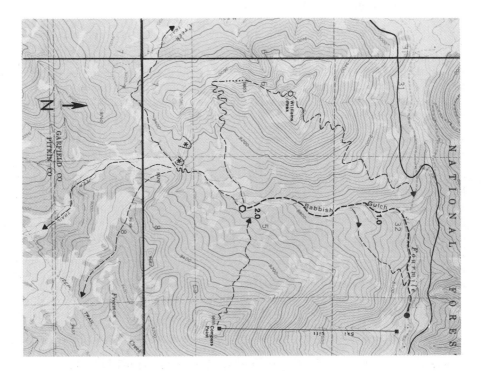

50 BEAVER CREEK AND FOURMILE PARK

Half-day and one day trips
Terrain: Easiest to more difficult
Distance: 1.5 miles/2.4 KM. one way
Skiing time: 1 hour one way
Elevation gain: 500 feet/152 M.
Maximum elevation: 9,460 feet/2,883 M.
Season: Early December through late March
Topographic map:
  U.S.G.S. Center Mountain, Colo. 1963
  U.S.G.S. Cattle Creek, Colo. 1961
  U.S.G.S. Stony Ridge, Colo. 1963
Sopris Ranger District
White River National Forest

Construction workers of the early Colorado Midland Railway named both the Threemile and Fourmile Creeks because these tributaries joined the Roaring Fork River three and four miles above Glenwood Springs. The Fourmile Creek Valley opens into half-mile-wide, rolling snowfields west of the Sunlight Ski Area and Babbish Gulch (No. 49) and provides some of the easiest ski touring terrain in the Carbondale and Glenwood Springs areas. In mid-winter cross-country trips can be routed through aspen groves along the southern reaches of Bald Mountain and through the conifer hillsides west of Beaver Creek where wind protection is best. With the milder weather in spring when a hard crust has formed on the snowpack, Fourmile Park becomes a huge play area — the ski touring equivalent of an ice skating rink — with easy-gliding trips in any direction and of any length. For a different and unforgettable experience, reserve the night of the full moon in March or early April for a midnight tour over the smooth and softly-lit snowfields.

The Beaver Creek Valley forms a southeasterly finger of Fourmile Park and like Babbish Gulch and Marion Gulch (No. 48), it offers access on an up-and-over trip into several other drainages. A superb, one-day tour, more difficult than the terrain in Fourmile Park but still within beginner capabilities, climbs through the valley bottom to a turnback point near a slight saddle at 1.5 miles, and then returns cross-country through the aspen-filled hillsides, following part of the course used for the new Rocky Mountain

Shuffle citizen's race. This trip is measured for the information capsule and described in detail below.

Drive on Colo. 82 to the south end of Glenwood Springs, turn right onto Grand Ave. and proceed 0.3 mile, then cross a bridge, turn left onto "117 Rd." and continue 1.5 miles to "116 Rd." Turn right (south), follow the main road toward the Sunlight Ski Area, then fork right onto the new Fourmile Creek Road after 8.9 miles where the ski area road proceeds straight and continue another 3.1 miles across Fourmile Creek to an orange gate. Drive 1.8 miles more to the inconspicuous junction with the Beaver Creek jeep trail, marked by a post near trees left, a good parking spot and starting point for tours through either Fourmile Park or Beaver Creek.

Drop left off the road and begin skiing at 134°/SSE to the right of the Beaver Creek basin. After nearly 0.3 miles swing slightly left to a 100°/ESE bearing and head toward the left side of a conifer-covered ridge which lies between willow-filled tributaries of Beaver Creek. Pick up a jeep-size roadcut in the trees and break into an open snowfield in another 40 yards where the aspen-covered, 10,079-foot top of Williams Peak shows at 38°/NE, the 9,855-foot "false summit" can be seen to the right, and beautiful hillsides of soft beige aspen, each ridgetop and valley a darker color, appear beyond Fourmile Park northwest. Continue the gradual climb in and out of tree clumps, dip through a small drainage at 0.8 mile, then climb more steeply, following a cross-country course on either side of the creekbed. Make a final looping climb along a roadcut left of Beaver Creek and come to a half-buried post-pole fence which marks the saddle at mile 1.5. Far below, Fourmile Park can be seen as a white spot among aspen hillsides.

For access to Babbish Gulch follow a 53°/ENE bearing along a Yank Creek tributary and ski through scenic double-topped spruce and fire-burned snags on a course marked occasionally with blue flagging. Pass the ruins of a log cabin in a conspicuous cluster of spruce after another 0.5 mile and break out onto a wide snowfield above the Babbish Gulch headwall. **To drop north into the gulch, do not ski the steep slopes of the headwall where avalanche danger is high but stay on a narrow, aspen-covered ridge and sidestep to less steep terrain.**

Nordic lesson

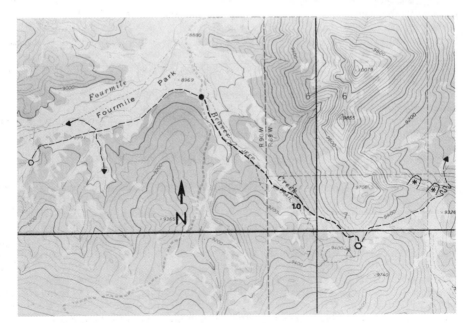

51 EAST BRUSH CREEK

One day trip
Terrain: Easiest
Distance: 5.9 miles /9.5 KM. one way
Skiing time: 3½-4½ hours one way
Elevation gain: 1,450 feet /442 M.
Maximum elevation: 9,070 feet /2,765 M.
Season: Mid-December through mid-March
Topographic maps:
  U.S.G.S. The Seven Hermits, Colo. 1962
  U.S.G.S. Fulford, Colo. 1962
Eagle Ranger District
White River National Forest

The tour route along the East Brush Creek Road east of Hardscrabble Mountain — not to be confused with Brush Creek and Pearl Pass (No. 33) near Crested Butte — heads east around the northern reaches of Adam Mountain toward Yeoman Park. Although few people know about this wilderness region northwest of the Sawatch Range, its anonymity may soon end: The proposed Adams Rib Ski Area super-development, if approved, would give the area immediate national notoriety. However, environmental studies through the Joint Review Process, including the Forest Service decision to designate a Winter Sports Site at Adam Mountain, will postpone any construction until 1982, possibly later. At that time the East Brush Creek Road will be plowed, bringing into one-day range a number of exciting destinations now reached only on two or three day winter camping trips. These sites include the old mining camp of Fulford northeast of Yeoman Park where as many as 600 people lived in the early 1900's, Fulford Cave — a spelunker's delight — in the upper East Brush Creek Valley, and timberline Mystic Island Lake at the East Brush Creek headwaters below the majestic, 13,043-foot Eagle Peak.

Drive on U.S. 6 to Eagle, turn south onto 5th Street and after five blocks turn right onto Capitol Street. Pass a sign directing travel to "Brush Creek," etc. at 6th Street, proceed onto Eagle Co. 307 and continue past turnoffs to the Salt Creek Road and Beecher Gulch to the East Brush Creek Road where a sign reads "Sylvan Lake 4," etc., 10.9 miles from

U.S. 6. Park along the roadside, or, if the East Brush Creek Road has been plowed, continue east to closure.

Ski east from snow closure on a gradual climb, passing tall cottonwood trees which surround the East Brush creekbed (right). Pass the ruins of a unique cabin with walls eleven logs high — still covered with a shingle roof — after 0.4 mile, ski by the prominent cut of Fisher Gulch on the Adam mountainside at 0.8 mile, and continue with easy, long glides to the Pipe Creek drainage at 1.7 miles. Here the rounded, white-topped New York Mountain shows at 102°/ESE on the skyline beyond the valley. Pass another unnamed gulch on Adam Mountain at 2.0 miles and ski under groves of stark aspen (left) which look like a beige cloud banked against the hillside. After 3.1 miles ski by a corral and turnoff to Triangle Park and swing right across East Brush Creek bridge, a possible goal for a one-day tour. Just before this crossing, the snowy summit of Charles Peak, topped with a slight cirque, appears above the forested range at 128°/SE.

Climb steadily on the aspen-lined roadbed through a series of curves (a fast, snaking drop on the return); cross No Name Creek at 3.5 miles, then re-cross East Brush Creek at 4.2 miles. Just beyond this last crossing the Old Fulford Trail forks left past a picturesque, three-story log cabin (private property). Climb gradually for another long mile as the valley narrows slightly, then drop to the willow-covered valley floor near the Yeoman Park Campground at 5.9 miles, another good turn-back point or camp spot.

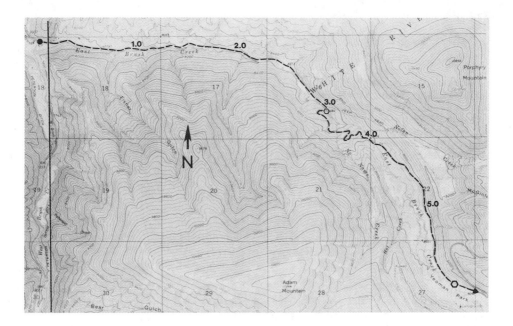

Water fill-up

52 EAST RIFLE CREEK

Half-day through overnight trips
Terrain: Easiest through most difficult
Distance: 9.9 miles/15.9 KM. one way
Skiing time: 5½-6½ hours one way
Accum. elevation gain: 2,620 feet/799 M.
Accum. elevation loss: 40 feet/12 M.
Maximum elevation: 9,460 feet/2,883 M.
Season: December through March
Topographic maps:
  U.S.G.S. Rifle Falls, Colo. 1966
  U.S.G.S. Triangle Park, Colo. 1966
Rifle Ranger District
White River National Forest

The tour through the East Rifle Creek Canyon ventures far into the grinding, roaring, whining, exhaust-filled territory of snowmobiles, the favorite weekend playground of one of the most active snowmobile clubs in the state. But as unappealing as this route at first sounds...and smells, other factors compensate for the internal combustion conflict. The wide, snow-packed East Rifle Creek roadbed provides the fastest and most direct southern access into the newly-designated Flat Tops Wilderness Area, an immense forest reserve of rolling mesa tops, sheer escarpments and deep valleys. And the access itself through the scenic East Rifle Creek Canyon makes good touring, especially with the quiet solitude during weekdays. Good stop-off points en route include the beautiful ice falls along the canyon walls after the 0.9 mile bridge, the chisled, shadowed rock walls which loom over the roadbed after 1.2 miles, and the intriguing, 10-foot-wide rocky entrance into the Little Box Canyon at 4.8 miles, each a photographer's paradise. The spacious snowfields of Triangle Park at the junction with the New Castle-Buford Road, measured for the information capsule, make a reasonable first-day goal for an extended trip.

To make an epic crossing of the Flat Tops Wilderness Area, little seen in the wintertime, proceed from Triangle Park on this suggested, experts-only route: northeast on the New Castle-Buford Road along a winding ridge to Trail 2340 (an escape route stays north on the New Castle-Buford Road, unplowed for over 16 miles to Buford), northeast via Trail 2340 toward Cliff Lakes, then north via Trail 1831 on a steep, 2,000-foot drop to South Fork Creek near the Wilderness Area boundary (another escape route exits down the South Fork Valley for over 12½ miles toward Buford). Ski east through South Fork Canyon via Trail 1827 to The Meadows, north on a rugged climb along Doe Creek onto the Flat Tops Plateau, then northeast via Trail 1825 past Twin Lakes, north on a daring drop via Trail 1819 through Big Fish Creek Valley to the North Fork White River (an escape route follows the sometimes snowmobile-packed North Fork Road west for about 15 miles to plowed road near the Lost Creek Guard Station). Continue northeast up Picket Pin Creek via Trail 1811 to a divide crossing west of West Lost Lake, north down the West Fork Williams Fork on Trails 1103 and 1116, southeast up East Fork Williams Fork on Trail 119, and northeast over the Pyramid Peak Range via Trail 117 to Sheriff Reservoir.

Follow the Sheriff Reservoir Road north to the Dunckley Pass Road/Rio Blanco Co. 8, then ski east on the final leg past the Chapman Reservoir turnoff to the plowed road near the Routt Co. 25 junction, following in reverse the Chapman Reservoir tour (No. 53) in *Northern Colorado Ski Tours*. This immense ski odyssey cuts southwest to northeast for about 94 miles through the Flat Tops Wilderness Area and surrounding White River and Routt National Forests and takes from eight to twelve days. Besides the published U.S.G.S. topo maps, obtain the essential advanced proofs — soon to be in the final stage 6 form — of unpublished maps ($1.25 each). For a free advance-proof index, write the U.S. Geological Survey, Topographic Division, Stop 510, Box 25046, Denver Federal Center, Denver, CO 80225.

Drive on I. 70 to Rifle, turn north onto Colo. 789/13 and proceed 3.3 miles to the junction with Colo. 325, marked by a sign reading "Rifle Gap Reservoir." Fork right, continue around the south side of the reservoir, then stay straight past the New Castle-Buford Road turnoff and enter the Rifle Gap Falls State Recreation Area. Proceed another 1.8 miles past the Rifle Falls Fish Hatchery to a parking spot near the Rifle Mtn. Park cattleguard, the usual point of road closure by mid-winter. Occasionally the road may be plowed or packed open through Rifle Mtn. Park for another 3.5 miles to the National Forest boundary.

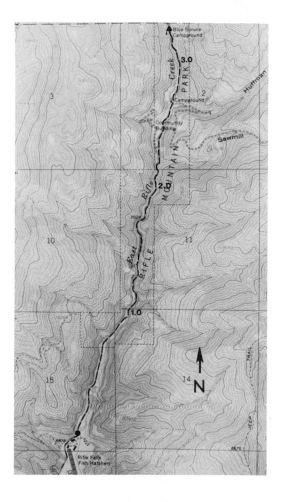

Ice Sculpture

53 WEST BENCH SKI TRAIL

One day trip
Terrain: More difficult
Distance: 3.2 miles/5.1 KM. one way
Skiing time: 1½-2 hours one way
Accum. elevation gain: 210 feet/64 M.
Accum. elevation loss: 200 feet/61 M.
Maximum elevation: 9,850 feet/3,002 M.
Season: Mid-November through early May
Topographic maps:
  U.S.G.S. Skyway, Colo. 1955
  U.S.G.S. Lands End, Colo. 1962
Collbran Ranger District
Grand Mesa National Forest

In comparison to touring trails throughout central Colorado, the West Bench Ski Trail north of the Grand Mesa rates as one of the finest for a variety of reasons. Despite only a 9,800-foot elevation, deep snow covers the trail by early winter and stays late into spring, as it does for all the Grand Mesa tours (No's. 53-58), assuring excellent ski conditions. The trail follows varied, interesting terrain — weaving through an aspen grove here, dropping down a small hillside there, cutting across an open clearing, then climbing slightly through a stand of spruce — all with an easily managed and nearly equal elevation gain and loss. And, unlike many of the other Grand Mesa touring areas, snowmobiles are banned from the trail by a Forest Service motor closure, in effect for the full trail length by 1977-78, which allows a ski track to be established between snowfalls and preserves the serenity of the tour.

The ski trail begins from the Colo. 65 highway and contours west along the West Bench plateau to the Powderhorn Ski Area, very much like the classic Hogan Park Ski Trail which links U.S. 40 on the Rabbit Ears Pass with the Steamboat Ski Area (*Northern Colorado Ski Tours* No. 60). Here are some of the tour variations: Rather than return on the West Bench Trail, ski the alpine slopes or ride down Lift No. 1 of the Powderhorn Ski Area (single ride ticket — $3). Or ride up Lift No. 1 and either ski the West Bench Trail "backwards" to Colo. 65 or proceed west along West Bench over a marked touring trail to Lift No. 2, a two-mile route used often as a

teaching area by ski touring instructors at the Powderhorn Ski Area. With a starting point at Colo. 65 or at the tops of Lifts No. 1 or No. 2, a popular extended tour best during the warm, windless days of April, proceeds west from Lift No. 2 through Picket Pass to the Grand Mesa top, and then follows the rim northwest across miles of open snowfields to Rapid Point, a trip of 3.5 miles from Lift No. 2, 8.7 miles from Colo. 65.

Drive on Colo. 65 to the northwest side of the Grand Mesa and proceed to the parking area marked "Mesa Lakes Ranger Station," etc. next to Jumbo Lake, 0.3 mile north of the Mesa Lakes Resort turnoff and 3.4 miles south of the Easter Seal Youth Camp turnoff. Additional parking can be found at the Mesa Lakes Resort (see No. 55). Note: The Colo. 65 highway is **not** maintained south of Mesa from 6 p.m. to 6 a.m. so take necessary precautions during stormy weather.

Ski west across the flat bed of Jumbo Reservoir, intercept a snow-covered roadbed beyond the reservoir dam, and loop south then west past Sunset Lake (left) toward the Mesa Lakes Ranger Station, well-marked by signs. Swing left below the Ranger Station across a bridge over Mesa Creek, soon curve north on a small road above stagnant ponds (right), passing several Ranger Station cabins. Turn left (west) in another hundred yards, make a steep but short shuss onto the Osborn Reservoir dam, the 0.8 mile mark, and continue the easy, rolling contour along the northeast-facing hillside, a delightful section to ski especially when the track has been set. Wind right then left through boulders and scattered spruce at 1.2 miles, following post markers. Pass an aspen-filled ravine and glide and climb over varied terrain through more and more aspen groves until breaking into the wide, flat "halfway park" at 1.7 miles. This spot, near the upper terminus of the old Grand Mesa Ski Area lift, serves often as a destination for a short, half-day tour.

Glide easily on a rolling, winding contour through scenic aspen, pass under another small boulder field, then break into a small meadow with a zig-zag fence at 2.5 miles and drop slightly on the conspicuous trail. Pass through more small clearings, eventually make a drop — fast if packed — through a grove of aspen, then break into a final, larger meadow and bend right to within sight of the bullwheel and counterweight of Lift No. 1, the 3.2 mile mark.

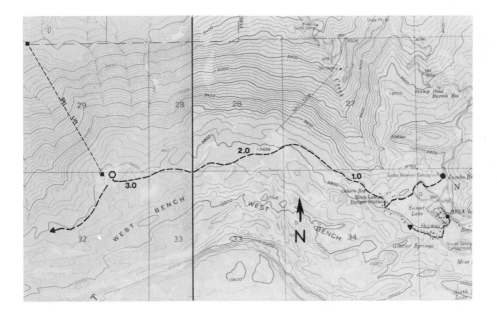

Training Session

54

WATER DOG, LONG SLOUGH, AND BULL CREEK RESERVOIRS

Half-day and one day trips
Terrain: Easiest to more difficult
Distance: 3.8 miles/6.1 KM. one way
Skiing time: 2-2½ hours one way
Accum. elevation gain: 320 feet/98 M.
Accum. elevation loss: 280 feet/85 M.
Maximum elevation: 9,980 feet/3,042 M.
Season: Mid-November through early May
Topographic map:
   U.S.G.S. Skyway, Colo. 1955
Collbran Ranger District
Grand Mesa National Forest

The tour along Water Dog, Long Slough, and Bull Creek Reservoirs passes through stark aspen groves and thickets of spruce, climbs and drops over knolls, and skirts vast parks and reservoir basins, terrain contrasts which add interest to the outing. With the help of a compass and map (the Grand Mesa National Forest Recreation Map has contour lines, covers more area, and costs less than the U.S.G.S. topos), any length trip can be routed cross-country through this territory. Possible destinations include Water Dog Reservoir at 0.5 mile, Long Slough Reservoir at 2.5 miles, and the Bull Creek Reservoir turnoff — measured for the information capsule — at 3.8 miles. By forking right (south) at the Bull Creek Reservoir turnoff, the tour can be extended past Bull Creek Reservoir No. 4 to the Lake of the Woods Trail and then looped west back to the Colo. 65 highway or continued east to Bonham Reservoir (see No. 56). Another excellent, longer route turns north at the Bull Creek Reservoir turnoff and links Bull Creek Reservoirs No. 3 and No. 2, then Cottonwood Lakes No. 2 and No. 1 to the Lake of the Woods Trail. Currently, unrestricted numbers of snowmobiles often travel these routes, mostly on weekends.

Drive on Colo. 65 to the parking area marked "Mesa Lakes Ranger Station," etc. next to Jumbo Lake on the northwest side of the Grand Mesa, 0.3 mile north of the Mesa Lakes Resort turnoff and 3.4 miles south of the Easter Seal Youth Camp turnoff. Additional parking can be found at the Mesa Lakes Resort (see No. 55).

Cross to the east side of the highway and begin skiing up the old Grand Mesa Road,

passing a sign which reads "Dead End Road 2 Miles." Pass over a cattle guard at the Forest Service gate after 0.2 miles, fork right in several more yards toward the "Water Dog Reservoir" where the old road drops north (a fun downhill tour itself, like the Easter Seal Camp Road), then climb steadily past Ball Reservoir No. 1 (left) and follow the rolling, often snowmobile-packed road to a rise above Water Dog Reservoir at 0.4 mile, a possible stopping point. To continue, cross the reservoir dam where the view extends right toward the steep north rim of the Grand Mesa. Reenter aspen on a slight climb, looping around a knoll left; begin a fast, thrilling descent through aspen then shady conifers after 1.1 miles, and enter a large meadow of rust and maroon willows. Bend right (northeast) to a crossing of Coon Creek at 1.7 miles, glide on a slight uphill grade to a saddle near mile 2.3, then continue through vast, open snowfields to a signpost at the mid-point along Long Slough Reservoir, the 2.7 mile mark and perhaps a turn-back point.

For a longer tour continue east above Long Slough Reservoir, pass aspen clumps right at 3.0 miles which mark the east end of the reservoir, then drop next to conifers on the right side of a park and pick up a trail-size cut near 3.4 miles. Proceed through trees on a winding, downhill course, soon bend left and enter a basin of willows which opens ahead and right. Ski by the inconspicuous Twin Basin Reservoir Trail turnoff at 3.6 miles, glide along the left side of another willow-filled park and come to the Bull Creek Reservoir turnoff at 3.8 miles, another good turn-back point.

Bustin' powder

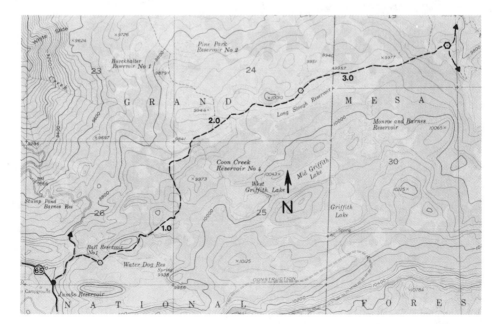

55 MESA LAKES SKI TRAILS

Half-day and one day trips
Terrain: Easiest through most difficult
Season: Mid-November through early May
Topographic map:
  U.S.G.S. Skyway, Colo. 1955
Collbran and Grand Junction Ranger Districts
Grand Mesa National Forest

A number of superb touring trails, some packed by daily use, others leading to unbroken powder fields, fan out from a trailhead hub at the Mesa Lakes Resort Lodge, a main center for cross-country skiing in the Grand Mesa area. Besides the trails described below, snowy roadbeds around the lodge make additional ski routes and lead to the Water Dog, Long Slough, and Bull Creek Reservoirs tour (No. 54) north of Jumbo Reservoir and to the West Bench Ski Trail (No. 53) at either Jumbo Reservoir or the Mesa Lakes Ranger Station. Another excellent tour route, the Grand Mesa Touring Classic Trail, begins from Colo. 65 south of Skyway Point (see map) and follows a partially-flagged loop of about 7 miles through parks and spruce stands on top of the Grand Mesa, terrain very similar to the Scales Lakes area (No. 57) farther east. In spring cross-country skiers race this scenic loop for the Grand Mesa Touring Classic citizen's race, sponsored by the Mesa Lakes Resort. For information on ski trails and lodging, contact: Mesa Lakes Resort, Mesa, CO 81643, telephone (303) 268-5467.

Drive on Colo. 65 to the northwest side of the Grand Mesa and continue to the Mesa Lakes Resort turnoff, 4.9 miles west of the Lands End turnoff and 5.6 miles east of the Powderhorn Ski Area turnoff. Turn south and proceed another 200 yards to the Mesa Lakes Lodge where limited parking can be found. Additional parking is available near Jumbo Reservoir (see No. 53). Be prepared with sand, shovel, and tire chains for the icy conditions on Colo. 65 during midwinter storms.

"Ski tourers live longer"

55A ANDERSON RESERVOIR NO. 2

Terrain: More difficult to most difficult
Distance: 2.8 miles/4.5 KM. one way
Skiing time: 2-2½ hours one way
Accum. elevation gain: 590 feet/180 M.
Accum. elevation loss: 60 feet/18 M.
Maximum elevation: 10,390 feet/3,167 M.

This trail winds west from Mesa Lake up a forested basin, then turns south at 2.0 miles on a steep climb up the north mesa rim and crosses windy snowfields to the Anderson Reservoir bowl. Look for tree clumps in a "W" pattern that mark the return trail back down the mesa rim.

55B LOST LAKE TRAIL

Terrain: Most difficult
Distance: 1.3 miles/2.1 KM. one way
Skiing time: 1-1½ hours one way
Accum. elevation gain: 380 feet/116 M.
Accum. elevation loss: 220 feet/67 M.
Maximum elevation: 10,180 feet/3,103 M.

Steep climbs and plunging return descents mark this trail to South Mesa Lake and Lost Lake, an especially deep bowl. Consider this tour on a cold, midwinter day when fresh powder snow blankets the ground.

55C MESA LAKE TRAIL

Terrain: Easiest
Distance: 1.5 miles/2.4 KM. round trip
Skiing time: 1 hour round trip
Accum. elevation gain: 100 feet/30 M.
Maximum elevation: 9,880 feet/3,011 M.

Of all the Mesa Lakes ski trails, the short loop around the large Mesa lakebed is most likely to be broken. It serves often as a training course for cross-country racers from the Grand Junction area.

55D OLD GRAND MESA ROAD

Terrain: Easiest
Distance: 2.3 miles/3.7 KM. one way
Skiing time: 1½ hours one way
Elevation gain: 640 feet/195 M.
Maximum elevation: 10,460 feet/3,188 M.

The old Grand Mesa roadbed leads east on a gradual climb to the mesa rim. For an easy trip, ideal for beginning skiers, start from Colo. 65, 1.0 miles up from the Lake of the Woods trailhead, and ski downhill to Mesa Lakes Resort. Other fun tours on the old Grand Mesa road begin from the tour route to Water Dog Reservoir (No. 54) and from the Easter Seal Camp Road.

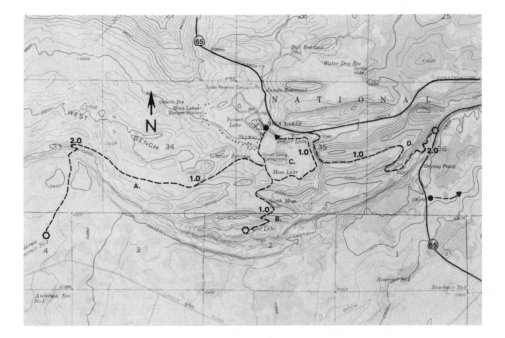

56 LAKE OF THE WOODS TRAIL

One day trip
Terrain: More difficult
Distance: 10.5 miles/16.9 KM. one way
Skiing time: 4-5 hours one way
Accum. elevation gain: 1,220 feet/372 M.
Accum. elevation loss: 1,570 feet/479 M.
Maximum elevation: 10,400 feet/3,170 M.
Season: Mid-November through early May
Topographic maps:
 U.S.G.S. Skyway, Colo. 1955
 U.S.G.S. Grand Mesa, Colo. 1955
  or:
 Grand Mesa National Forest
 Recreation Map
Collbran Ranger District
Grand Mesa National Forest

Water stop

The Lake of the Woods Trail stays below the north rim of the Grand Mesa and links several snow-blanketed parks and reservoir beds on a course with more sweeping drops and rolling climbs than the other Grand Mesa tours. At mile 5.0 on the north side of Cottonwood Lake No. 1 the trail meets the wide, often-packed Cottonwood Lakes Road which leads east on a fast climb and drop over the Horse Mountain Range to a pick-up point at Bonham Reservoir, an adventurous trip of 10.5 total miles as figured for the information capsule. However, the Colorado Division of State Parks has recently begun to grade the snowpack from Bonham Reservoir to Cottonwood Lake No. 1 for a snowmobile trail which does detract from the skiing experience. Contact the Regional Parks Manager, Box B, Palisade, CO 81526, telephone (303) 464-7297 for current information.

Drive on Colo. 65 to the northwest side of the Grand Mesa and proceed to the Lake of the Woods Trail junction at the end of the long switchback below the mesa rim, 2.0 miles east of the Mesa Lakes Resort turnoff and 2.9 miles north of the Lands End turnoff. Park in the plowed area 150 yards north of the unplowed jeep road. For a drop-off or pick-up at the Bonham Reservoir, turn south at Collbran onto the "National Forest Access"

road, then fork left after 2.0 miles at the KE Road/58½ Road junction. Proceed past the Big Creek Cow Camp at 11.3 miles and come to road closure and parking at the reservoir, 12.1 miles from Collbran.

Pick up a snowy jeep road — many times broken with a hard-set track — to the south of the meadow near the parking area, glide through a section of thick spruce and fir, then bend left and drop and climb through a basin. Continue east-northeast on a drop into a large, U-shaped clearing at 0.3 mile, bear toward the opening on the right, then follow blazed trees on a long, thrilling downhill run through tall spruce, eventually spilling into another clearing near 0.8 mile. Cross the clearing on a 56°/NE bearing, staying right of a small mound, cross a creek and make a winding climb through trees to a trail junction at mile 1.2. The trail to Bull Creek Reservoir No. 4 forks left (north) here and provides an access to Water Dog, Long Slough, and Bull Creek Reservoirs (No. 54) while the Lake of the Woods Trail branches right (east).

Wind south then east, passing a small clearing; soon bear northeast along the narrow Lake of the Woods and continue through fun dips and rolls to a downhill onto Bull Basin No. 1 at 1.7 miles. Ski to the left of the dam on Bull Creek Reservoir No. 2 at 2.0 miles, pass

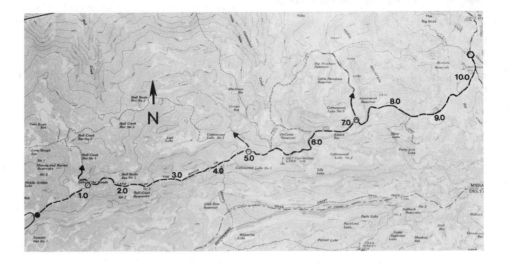

along the north side of Bull Creek Reservoir No. 1 and make an easy climb to the "High Line" park at mile 2.7. Re-enter the trees on a climb right then left after 3.6 miles and follow the blazed trail through small meadows, eventually dropping steeply onto the open hillside at mile 3.9. Follow post markers on a downhill traverse past the Cottonwood Lakes Trail turnoff at mile 4.1, drop through more snowfields — good terrain for christie and telemark turns — beneath chimney ruins which mark the cabin sites shown on the map at 4.4 miles, and glide over or north of the vast bed of Cottonwood Lake No. 1 to the Cottonwood Lakes Road at mile 5.0.

For the longer trip to Bonham Reservoir, follow the wide, packed roadbed east on an easy drop past the Cottonwood Lake No. 4 turnoff at 5.7 miles, swing north then east past Kitson Reservoir at mile 6.4, and fork right where the road to Neversweat Reservoir turns left at 7.1 miles. Curve left (north) on a long, gradual climb to a saddle in the Horse Mountain Range at mile 7.7 from which the 11,236-foot summit of Leon Peak can be seen at 84°/E. Make a gradual drop past the Silver Lake Turnoff at 8.5 miles, continue the rolling descent along the Silver Lake creekbed (right), then pass the south end of the snow-filled Bonham Reservoir at 9.5 miles and end the tour at Bonham Campground, the 10.5 mile mark.

57 SCALES LAKES AREA

Half-day and one day trips
Terrain: Easiest
Distance: 1.8 miles/2.9 KM. one way
Skiing time: 1 hour one way
Elevation loss: 45 feet/14 M.
Maximum elevation: 10,830 feet/3,301 M.
Season: Mid-November through early May
Topographic map:
   U.S.G.S. Skyway, Colo. 1955
Grand Junction Ranger District
Grand Mesa National Forest

Interlaced drainageways and stands of penetrable spruce around Scales Lakes atop the Grand Mesa create an ideal situation for a ski touring trail system similar to those developed by the Forest Service in the Pikes Peak, South Park, Leadville and Holy Cross Ranger Districts. Even without trail markers, cross-country loops can easily be made with the aid of the U.S.G.S. Skyway topo and a compass, as suggested on the map photo. One main trail, figured for the information capsule and described below, begins from the county line parking area and heads north along a snow-buried summer road to a radio relay station, following orange/black poles which also guide the radio maintenance crews. The fact that this trail is marked increases ski traffic and thus results often in a fast, hard track with no orienteering complications, ideal skiing conditions much like the West Bench Ski Trail (No. 53). Although snowmobilers prefer the Lands End Road and adjacent mesa top to the south, no motor restrictions exist currently in this area. For more information, contact the Grand Junction Ranger District, Federal Building, 4th and Rood, Grand Junction, CO 81501, telephone (303) 242-8211.

By skiing northeast from the relay station the tour can be looped through a wide drainageway to the mesa rim. This point looks down the steep, rocky escarpment over 700 feet to the many glacier-carved lakes around the Grand Mesa Resort, giving a good perspective of the unusual geology of the area. Millions of years ago waters of a great lake rippled over the area that is now the Grand Mesa. During the Tertiary Period — the same time span as the dramatic Laramide Orogeny when the Rocky Mountain chain was thrust up from Alaska to New Mexico — volcanic lava began to ooze through cracks in the rock beneath the lake, forming layers of erosion-resistant material that would become the cap rock of the mesa. About 20 million years ago the volcanic action ceased, rivers began eroding away the softer material over the mesa, subsequent glaciers scoured the many depressions where the lava cap had broken and slipped. Thus today the Grand Mesa, one of the largest flat-topped mountains in the world, rises almost a mile above the surrounding countryside and is surrounded by dozens of lakes.

Drive on Colo. 65 to the Mesa County/Delta County boundary near the southeast rim of the Grand Mesa, 1.5 miles east of the Lands End Road junction, and park in the plowed area along the side of the highway. Note: The Colo. 65 highway is **not** maintained over Grand Mesa from 6 p.m. to 6 a.m. so take necessary precautions during stormy weather.

Ski north from the parking area, keeping the main body of spruce on the right. Either pick up a trail in the middle of the wide drainage, marked with orange triangles, or for more shelter from wind, ski cross-country through trees east of the drainage. Pass the "10,810" park which opens right at 0.3 mile, continue north through a narrower opening after 0.9 mile, and come to two excellent alternate routes in another 300 yards: one turns left (west) and follows an unnamed drainage for 1.7 miles to Reservoir No. 8, and the other turns right and crosses Scales Lake No. 1. To continue to the relay station, follow the markers past the west end of Scales Lake, a point which gives view to the relay station above the trees at 25°/NE. Bend right along treeline to an opening in the conifers at 1.3 miles, then turn left, ski through a shady cut for 70 yards, and continue over open snowfields toward the high, conspicuous steel tower, the 1.8 mile mark. Other loop trails fan out from the tower: a flat, fast route follows Kahnah Creek for 2.2 miles to Reservoir No. 8, a northeasterly route leads to the mesa rim in 1.5 miles, and another route heads east and southeast across Scales Lakes No. 2 (see map).

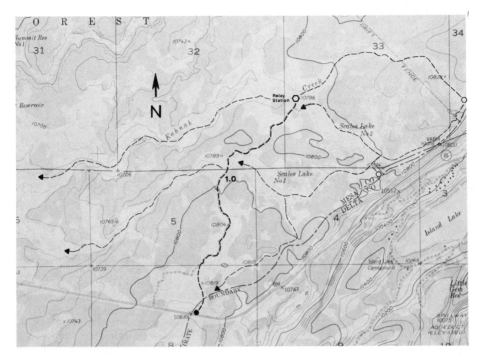

Snowfield crossing

58 COUNTY LINE
JUMPOFF

Half-day trip
Terrain: Easiest to more difficult
Distance: 3.6 miles /5.8 KM. round trip
Skiing time: 2-2½ hours round trip
Accum. elevation gain: 210 feet/64 M.
Maximum elevation: 10,850 feet /3,307 M.
Season: Mid-November through early May
Topographic map:
 U.S.G.S. Skyway, Colo. 1955
Grand Junction Ranger District
Grand Mesa National Forest

For the person just getting started in ski touring, the easy, half-mile tour from the "county line jumpoff" on Grand Mesa to a vista point on the southeast rim provides the perfect introduction to the sport. The cross-country route, often marked with ski tracks, allows long, leisurely glides over the flats and gentle coasts down the backsides of knolls, "easiest" terrain but with enough variety for interesting skiing. And the vista, a special highlight of the tour, looks down into glacier-carved lakebeds over 800 feet below, giving a good appreciation for the unusual Grand Mesa geomorphology, and then scans hazy, flat-topped mesas in the Uncompahgre Plateau over 45 miles away.

With a bit of fun orienteering a loop tour can be made, as figured for the information capsule and shown on the map photo. The loop follows the rim southwest for another mile or so from the vista point, then holds a westerly bearing around hillocks and through stands of spruce to a vast, hard-to-miss basin, a splendid touring area except on windy days. After re-entering the trees at the north end of the basin, the route maintains an easterly bearing to the parking area. Although there is currently no closure to motorized vehicles on Grand Mesa (with the recent exception of the West Bench Ski Trail No. 53), this loop tour stays in a corner usually not used by snowmobilers who favor the Lands End Road and adjoining snowfields farther west.

Drive on Colo. 65 to the Mesa County/Delta County boundary near the southeast rim of the Grand Mesa, 1.5 miles east of the Lands End Road junction, and park in the plowed area on the south side of the highway. Note: The Colo. 65 highway is **not** maintained over the Grand Mesa from 6 p.m. to 6 a.m. so take necessary precautions during stormy weather.

Ski south from the parking area through snowfields dotted with spruce (shown as white on the topo). Begin veering to the left (southeast) after several hundred yards where the trees are most scattered and weave around slight knolls until reaching the mesa rim. From a lookout at 0.5 mile, marked by a post, an encompassing panorama spreads across the horizon. Grand Mesa mountains show east-southeast beyond the rim, snowy, flat-topped peaks mark the mountain range beyond Paonia east-southeast, and across the often smoke-filled Delta basin the hazy, blue Uncompahgre Plateau comes into view southwest.

To make a loop tour, use the rim for a bearing but stay about one hundred yards back from the edge to avoid rocky hillocks, steep ridges, and other obstacles, and proceed on a contour through dense timber. Cross a large meadow at 0.7 mile, then cross another at 1.0 mile which fans out from a drainageway right, and continue the winding, cross-country course west-southwest through more stands of conifers, terrain which produces a feeling of quiet concealment and protection. Swing right after breaking into a small meadow near 1.4 miles, follow a compass bearing of about 278°/WNW through spruce clumps and clearings until hitting a vast, open basin at 1.9 miles. Follow to the left of treeline, heading north then northeast into the narrowing basin; funnel into the trees — accurately represented on the topo — at 2.8 miles and again hold a compass bearing of about 75°/E for the final 0.8 mile to the open snowfields above the parking area.

Telemark turns

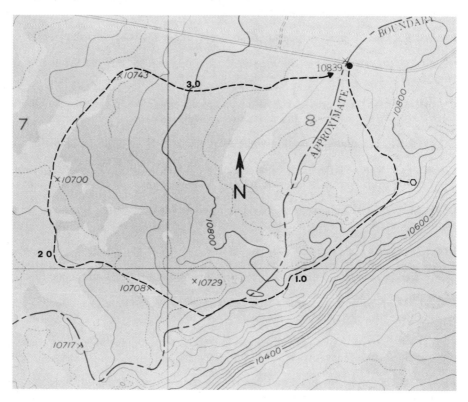

GLOSSARY

ALPINE LIFE ZONE: This zone begins at timberline (about 11,500 feet) and extends to the highest mountain peaks. Low temperatures and high winds create a climate similar to that beyond the Arctic Circle. The wind-packed snowfields cover the grasses, sedges, and dwarf shrubs until late May or June.

AVALANCHE: The "hard slab" avalanche, common along the Front Range, occurs when heavy deposits of wind-drifted snow form on top of unstable bases. The hollow sound of snow drumming or cracking under the skis is one sign of this extremely dangerous condition.

BEARING: The straight line of travel or sight, fixed in relation to the direction north.

BLAZED TRAIL: A trail marked by Forest Service personnel by chipping a small cut above a large cut into the bark of conspicuous trees.

BLUE SPRUCE: A medium-sized tree with stiff, prickly needles, 1-1½ inches long, silvery-blue color; has light brown cones over 3 inches long; generally found below 9,000 feet elevation along creeks or ponds.

BREAK TRAIL: To push through new snow, setting a TRACK for following skiers.

CHINOOK WIND: A warm, dry wind that occasionally descends the Front Range mountains, decreasing the snow cover quickly.

CLEAR-CUTTING: A term used by foresters to describe the logging practice of cutting all the trees on a slope, in contrast to selective cutting.

CONTOUR: To maintain elevation while following the curve of a mountainside.

CROSS-COUNTRY SKIING: As opposed to SKI TOURING, the competitive Nordic sport of racing over a specially prepared TRACK, using light, fragile skis and light boots.

DOUBLE POLE: To achieve forward momentum by planting both ski poles in unison for a propelling push.

DOUGLAS FIR: The common "Christmas tree" with soft, flat needles, 1-1½ inches long, which stick out in all directions from the branch; has cones conspicuous with three-pronged bracts extending beyond scales; found between 8,000 and 9,000 feet.

ENGLEMANN SPRUCE: A tree with prickly needles, 1 inch long; has cones 1-1½ inches long with papery scales; found mostly above 9,000 feet.

FALL LINE: A term used by skiers to describe the angle or course down a mountainside with the fastest drop in elevation.

FLAT TRACK: A prepared TRACK on level terrain where a beginning skier can practice weight shifts, and poling techniques.

138

FROST-WEDGING: A process of erosion where water runs into rock seams, expands with freezing, and cracks off bits of rock.

GLIDE: To propel oneself forward by sliding one ski at a time, each stride initiated by a "kick" from the weighted ski.

GORP: A high calorie trail snack or emergency food, usually a mixture of nuts, M&Ms, and raisins. Good!

HERRINGBONE: To climb by keeping the ski tips apart, tails together, and ankles turned in, and stepping into the fall line.

HYPOTHERMIA: The gradual lowering of body temperature due to exposure and exhaustion, leading to stupor, collapse, and eventual death.

KLISTER: A very soft wax applied to the ski bottom for icy and slushy snow conditions, usually needed only in the late spring in Colorado.

LIMBER PINE: A soft pine with needles in clusters of five, 1½-3 inches long; becomes twisted and dwarfed in exposed locations; grows in dry, rocky soil, often near timberline.

LODGEPOLE PINE: A hard pine with stiff, dark green needles in clusters of two, 1-3 inches long has scaly bark of black to light brown color, found between 8,000 and 10,000 feet.

MONTANE LIFE ZONE: This zone lies between 8,000 and 10,000 feet and produces thick forests of lodgepole pine, aspen and spruce. Snow usually remains through the winter on shady north-facing slopes but can melt clear between snowstorms in open meadows and south-facing slopes.

MORAINE: An accumulation of earth and rock debris deposited by a glacier.

PINE TAR: A pine distillate applied to the ski bottom before wax to seal the wood from moisture and to hold the wax better.

PONDEROSA PINE: A hard pine with dark, yellow-green needles in clusters of two or three, 3-7 inches long; has dark bark when young, reddish-orange bark when mature; grows 150 to 180 feet tall.

POWDER SNOW: A fluffy, dry snow that creates ideal skiing conditions, formed with colder temperatures.

SHUSS: To ski quickly downhill with few or no turns; to "downhill."

SIDESTEP: To climb or drop by keeping skis perpendicular to the fall line, moving one ski forward and sideways, then bringing the other ski alongside.

SKI CROSS-COUNTRY: To pick the most logical route where no roads or trails exist.

SKI TOURING: As opposed to CROSS-COUNTRY SKIING, the recreational sport of exploring the "backcountry," using strong, medium-weight skis and higher cut boots; the winter counterpart to summer hiking.

SKI MOUNTAINEERING: The winter sport characterized by steep climbs and long descents, using heavy skis and stiff climbing boots.

SNOW PLOW: To reduce speed or stop by spreading the tails of the skis, bending knees and turning ankles inward to set edges.

SNOWPLOW TURN: To change direction on a downhill run by assuming the SNOW PLOW position and shifting weight to the ski opposite the direction of the turn; used in packed snow or unbreakable crust.

STEP TURN: To change direction on a downhill run by picking up one ski, pointing it in the direction of the turn, shifting weight onto it and bringing the other ski alongside.

SUB-ALPINE FIR: A small tree with soft, flat needles, 1-1½ inches long, crowded toward the upperside of the branch; has purple, erect cones, 2-4 inches long; found at timberline often with englemann spruce. Also called Alpine Fir.

SUB-ALPINE LIFE ZONE: This zone ranges from 10,000 feet to timberline (about 11,500 feet) and contains small, compact tree groups rather than unbroken forests. Dependable snow cover for skiing usually exists here from December through April.

TELEMARK: To provide stability for straight, downhill running over uneven terrain by extending one ski forward, bending both knees, and distributing weight equally between both skis.

TELEMARK TURN: To change direction on a downhill run by assuming a TELEMARK position, then turning the forward ski inward at a steadily widening angle; used in breakable crust and deep snow.

TIMBERBASH: To make a downhill run through thick timber, sometimes on purpose.

TOPO MAP: A graphic representation of part of the earth's surface, showing the location and shape of mountains, valleys, and plains, the network of streams and rivers, and selected manmade features.

TRACK: The parallel path of skis in snow, usually about 8 inches apart; the race course in CROSS-COUNTRY SKIING.

TRAVERSE: To ascend or descend a hill at an angle to the FALL LINE.

WAX: A substance applied to the ski bottom to allow the ski to both glide and grip on the snow.

WEDEL: To link short turns in a rhythmical way.

WHITE FIR: A pale pea-green tree with soft, flat needles, 2-3 inches long; has pale-green to purple, erect cones, 3-5 inches long; found on hillsides with ponderosa pine and douglas fir, and in canyons with blue spruce.

WIND CHILL: The combined cooling power of low temperature, wind, and humidity.

WIND-SCOURED: The condition of an open park, meadow, or road that has been stripped bare of snow by excessive wind.

WHITE-OUT: The loss of depth perception or total loss of visibility during blizzard conditions.